Taking Action with Teacher Research

Edited by
Ellen Meyers and
Frances O'Connell Rust

HEINEMANN
Portsmouth, NH

Heinemann

361 Hanover Street
Portsmouth, NH 03801–3912
www.heinemann.com

Offices and agents throughout the world

Teachers featured in the front cover photos are:
  Matt Wayne (upper left)
  Natasha Warikoo (middle)
  Laura Goldstone (bottom photo)

Library of Congress Cataloging-in-Publication Data
Taking action with teacher research / edited by Ellen Meyers and
  Frances O'Connell Rust.
      p.   cm.
    Includes bibliographical references.
    ISBN 0-325-00544-3
    1. Action research in education.   I. Meyers, Ellen.   II. Rust,
Frances O'Connell.

LB1028.24 .T35 2003
370'.7'2—dc21   2002190840

Editor: Lois Bridges
Production editor: Sonja S. Chapman
Cover design: Jenny Jensen Greenleaf
Cover photographer: Kristine Larsen
Typesetter: House of Equations, Inc.
Manufacturing: Steve Bernier

Printed in the United States of America on acid-free paper
12 11   VP   9 10

Contents

Foreword

Adam Urbanski

When it comes to the education of students, nothing matters more than the knowledge, skills, and attitudes of teachers. And when it comes to improving teaching, teachers' knowledge and collective wisdom can make the difference between random acts of innovation and real reforms.

Taking Action with Teacher Research offers indispensable insights into the hurdles that currently undermine more effective teaching and learning. This book points us in promising directions for overcoming such obstacles as lack of resources, excessive school and class sizes, lack of involvement, and lack of meaningful learning opportunities for teachers. *Taking Action with Teacher Research* is a lucid guide to identifying problems in classrooms, schools, and beyond, asking questions, designing and implementing research to find answers, and using the data to effect promising change. Every chapter contains rich examples of teacher leadership in action.

When teachers consider themselves to be researchers, not just consumers of research, they are exercising leadership. When teachers write about their teaching and about their professional work, they are exercising teacher leadership. And when teachers form networks to share their knowledge and work, they are breaking down the formidable obstacles that have thwarted teacher leadership for so many decades.

There are many reasons why teachers, historically, have not assumed appropriate leadership roles in schools and in education. For one thing, there has been a confusion of the meaning of leadership with that of management, supervision, and administration. That's because teachers inherited an unquestioned acquiescence to a system that legitimized managerial authority. Like administrators, teachers became accustomed to hierarchical organizations and conceded decision-making and leadership functions to their supervisors.

Historically, "professional" teachers were expected to obey their superiors, not to question authority, and to view their calling as a vocation—not primarily a career. "Poverty, chastity, and obedience" were the standards—much as in a convent. A "good" teacher was expected to stay in the classroom and teach the students no less than a "good woman" was expected to stay at home and take care of the children. Hence, any teacher aspiring to leadership, school-wide or beyond, became vulnerable to the accusation that she was "abandoning her kids." Moreover, full-time engagement in the classroom left little time or energy—never mind legitimacy—for communication, influence, or leadership. Lack of a culture and traditions that would serve to empower teachers has created an expectation that the only job of teachers is to teach students and to consider the classroom as the legitimate extent of their influence.

The very structure of the system worked against development of teacher leadership. The closer you were to the classroom, for example, the less you were paid. Scheduling left little room for collegiality and contact. And lack of access to new knowledge made teachers ever dependent on "experts" who were nonteachers or, at best, were former teachers.

All along, teachers deplored the ramifications of such lack of access, lack of voice, and lack of collaboration. Many still lament that they "love to teach, but hate the job."

Frustration, along with the lack of democratic dynamics in schools, has taken its toll. Some learned to cope by honing their skills in creative insubordination. They followed their conscience and their moral imperative to do right by their students even if it meant "complying differently." They pursued reforms without permission. They did lesson plans that would satisfy their supervisors, but often these plans had little to do with what they actually did in the classroom (except, of course, during formal observations). In other words, some led dual lives. This duplicity eventually became second nature—an expected aspect of a teacher's existence. All it required is blocking the little window in the classroom door with a sheet of paper, perhaps with a display of a student's work. Instant privacy. And, for the sake of such "autonomy" in their own classrooms, teachers sacrificed their prospects for influence at the school level and beyond.

Still others chose a different path. They internalized it all, and became proponents and guardians of their own disempowerment. For them, the proletarian culture of sameness was at least predictable and survivable. So any teacher who deviated from it became a target of colleagues. "Who do you think you are?" was often the message from teachers themselves to any fellow teacher who would show interest or leadership that exceeded these expected parameters. Raising school-wide issues, commenting on matters of policy, or questioning the performance of other teachers had a "citizen's arrest" ring to it. Somehow, the lack of perceived legitimacy put such attempts at initiative into question and under suspicion: "Is he a turncoat, traitor, troublemaker . . . ?" This greatly hampered the prospects for advancing teacher leadership.

Leaders are those among us who unlock our individual and collective potential, increase informed choices for us, and inspire us to aspire to more. And while there can be many manifestations of this, it all leads to a common, bottom-line purpose: to increase the chances that more students learn better.

Teacher leadership is also indispensable to the task of building a more genuine profession for current and future teachers. As now structured, the teaching occupation lacks the essential features of a real profession. To change all this, teachers must play the leading role in bringing about the essential aspects of a more genuine profession:

- *Shared knowledge base.* All professionals must possess knowledge that is not common to those not in the profession. In teaching, that means that teachers should know their subjects well (content knowledge); how to teach effectively to all students (pedagogy); how learning occurs; and how children and adolescents develop.
- *Standards.* High and rigorous standards of practice must be well known and they must be enforced—especially through

peer review, since no one knows the difference between good teaching and bad teaching better than the best teachers themselves.

- *Internship*. New practitioners should be inducted into the profession under the guidance of more experienced and expert colleagues who would serve as mentors to them. No novice should have to learn by trial and error, through sink or swim.
- *Differentiated roles*. The "sameness" in teaching must yield to appropriate matching of the practitioners' work with their particular stage in the profession, their expertness, and their experience. What we euphemistically refer to as "the most challenging assignments," for example, should not be relegated to the least experienced and most vulnerable colleagues. And along with differentiated staffing, we should have differentiated status, responsibilities, and compensation.
- *Professional discretion*. A hallmark of any profession is that the professionals are trusted to practice without excessive supervision. Teachers must be viewed as competent to make their own decisions about teaching. They should have ample access to expert advice without the automatic expectation to substitute others' judgment for their own.
- *Promotion within the profession*. It should be possible to promote teachers in the profession without compelling them to leave teaching altogether. Joining the ranks of administrators should be by choice, not by default.
- *Accountability*. As in any other genuine profession, accountability should be first and foremost to those served, not to those to whom one reports. Teachers, therefore, should be accountable for knowing and meeting high and rigorous standards of practice; for putting the needs of their students first; and, as Linda Darling-Hammond advocates, for continuously reflecting on the impact of their teaching and adjusting their practice based on that information.

In addition to teaching students, and not in lieu of it, teachers like those who contributed to this volume, can assume leadership roles to advance their profession and to improve teacher and student learning. As you will read here, they can serve as mentors to new teachers, coaches to each other, peer evaluators, members of team-teaching groups, and interveners who assist colleagues lacking competency. Teachers can also write curricula, design professional development opportunities, write and speak about teaching and learning, conduct research in education and content areas, and demonstrate for others more accomplished teaching practice.

Taking Action with Teacher Research provides examples of teacher leadership. A revolution of rising expectations has inspired teachers to aspire to more—for themselves and for their students. These exceptional examples could become the norm.

What teachers have envisioned for themselves, for their students, and for their schools, can become a reality if ever increasing numbers of teachers actively work toward that vision and commit for the long haul. They must expand the conversations, accelerate collaborative efforts, and find ways as these teachers have done to become agents of change.

Adam Urbanski is president of the Rochester (NY) Teachers Association, a vice-president of the American Federation of Teachers, and director of the Teacher Union Reform Network (TURN) of AFT and NEA Locals.

Acknowledgments

We wish to thank our colleagues at Teachers Network and New York University Steinhardt School of Education for their leadership, commitment, support, input, and help with this work: Ellen Dempsey, president and CEO, Teachers Network; Mark Zvonkovic, chairperson, Teachers Network; Charlotte K. Frank, vice president, Teachers Network; Ann Marcus, dean, Steinhardt School of Education, New York University; Mark Alter, chair, Department of Teaching and Learning, Steinhardt School of Education, New York University; Sybil Jacobson, president and CEO, MetLife Foundation; Peter Paul, program director, Teachers Network; Norm Fruchter, director, Institute for Education and Social Policy, New York University; Corey Todaro, program associate, Teachers Network; Polly Lagana, JP Morgan/ Chase intern, Teachers Network; Roberto Martinez, graduate advisor, Department of Teaching and Learning, Steinhardt School of Education, New York University; and Erin Smith, program officer, MetLife Foundation.

Support for the Teachers Network Policy Institute is made possible by grants from the MetLife Foundation, the John S. and James L. Knight Foundation, the Rockefeller Foundation, the Booth Ferris Foundation, and the Rita J. and Stanley H. Kaplan Family Foundation.

We also wish to give special thanks to our editor, Lois Bridges, and to all MetLife Fellows past and present.

Introduction

Frances O'Connell Rust and Ellen Meyers

This book is about the reality of schools and the forces that teachers, children, and their parents are up against in trying to make public education successful. This is a story that tells of hope and hard work. It is instructive for policymakers who are interested in improving student achievement. Like most true stories, it is complex.

While there are many factors that make the reform of public schools a challenge, we have chosen to focus on three, which our research illuminates: resources needed to meet standards, conditions of the workplace, and the status of the teaching profession. When listening to teachers, those who work most closely with our children, these are the issues that surface.

In many urban and rural schools, the lack of resources required to meet standards is a fact of life, and for many children, this is a double whammy. Each day, they leave one impoverished environment for another. The impact of these underresourced environments places enormous stress on these children, their parents, and their teachers. They are pressed to meet the same high standards as their environment-rich suburban neighbors; however, they lack the resources and experiences that will enable them to do so.

Compounding the issue of inadequate resources are the conditions of the workplace where time, class size, and support are structured in ways that do not allow children and teachers opportunities to develop relationships integral to successful teaching and learning. Inflexible schedules, overcrowded schools and classrooms, and professional isolation prohibit creative, sustained thinking on the part of children and adults.

The low status of teachers in the educational hierarchy as well as in the eyes of the public is crippling to school reform. Teachers in urban and rural schools do not have parity in pay scale with their suburban counterparts and often have little or no say in instructional choices, material selections, and professional development. This leads to disempowerment and disenchantment among teachers and high turnover in the profession.

The Teachers' Voice

Our book brings the voice of inquiry-oriented teachers into the policy discussion of school reform. It draws from a unique set of action research studies completed over the past four years by one hundred teachers across the country—MetLife Fellows in the Teachers Network Policy Institute. The studies we chose for this book are representative of the whole in that they draw attention to the complex and delicate interaction that is teaching and learning, and to the implicit link between teachers' actions and student achievement. This set of studies focuses specifically on the way that policy plays out in urban classrooms and schools around the issues of resources, conditions, and teaching status. They not only give us a deeper understanding of the complex factors that shape teacher and student interactions, but also provide us with remedies.

Jane Ching Fung (Chapter 3) focuses on the conditions of schooling and the status of teachers. She did her research in an elementary school near downtown Los Angeles where over 55 percent of the teachers were noncredentialed and had taught for less than three years. The study examines the impact of ongoing collaboration within a teacher network on new teachers' understanding and use of state language arts standards in classroom practice and new teacher retention.

Two studies are situated in middle schools in New York City's Community School District No. 2. Both make the case that even in a high-performing urban school district, the issues of inadequate resources and depressing conditions can hinder children's achieving standards. Lara Goldstone (Chapter 4), teaching in Chinatown, looked at obstacles to successful communication with the parents of her students. Missing in this setting were access to translators, time for parent-teacher conferences, and the availability of bilingual materials. In a Lower East Side middle school, Matt Wayne (Chapter 2) confronted the problem of getting appropriate books into the hands of eight struggling readers. The issues here were how to gain access to additional resources and teacher empowerment.

Urban high schools are particularly resistant to reform. Three of the studies we included demonstrate how difficult it is to enact reform measures at this level. Like Matt Wayne, Carol Tureski (Chapter 5) at International High School in Queens found that the lack of high-interest, culturally relevant resources presented a significant obstacle to facilitating adolescent literacy. She and her colleagues experienced barriers to effective teaching due to their lack of involvement in decision-making around scheduling, instruction, and resources. Janet Price (Chapter 7) conducted a second study at International High School in Queens. Because the high school served non-English-speaking immigrants, Price and her colleagues wanted to develop an assessment process that would clearly demonstrate student progress. Her study shows what can happen when teachers are able to set the professional development agenda for their school.

Natasha Warikoo (Chapter 6) at Manhattan International High School looked at the impact of class size on her teaching of second-language learners in her math classes. She found that with smaller classes, she could reach individual students more easily and could tailor her whole-group instruction to better meet the needs of all of her students.

The unique character of each of these studies provides insight about the complexity of teaching. Their individuality also helps to uncover some of the ways in which education policy intersects and shapes practice in classrooms and in schools.

Classroom Inquiry and Education Policy

Each of these studies grew out of teachers' questions regarding the implementation of some aspect of education policy as it plays out in their schools and classrooms. These studies were conducted as part of the ongoing work of the Teachers Network Policy Institute. From the beginning, the mission of TNPI has been to give teachers an active voice in education policymaking so that education mandates are informed by the realities of daily classroom life and are aimed at improving the condition of our nation's schools and producing real results in student learning.

For our inquiry, we use action research. We understand action research both as the essential activity of a reflective teacher and as a viable means for teachers to identify how their practice is improving student achievement. In the first sense of action research, we think of the questions that guide the activities that teachers engage in every day: Who is paying attention? Who seems engaged? Who is having trouble? How am I doing? How can I work more effectively? In the second sense, our work has shown us that when teachers question their practice and gather and analyze data using tools easily incorporated into everyday teaching, improvement of practice is a logical outcome.

To answer the questions that they shape, the teachers draw on research tools that are often already part of their teaching repertoire but which they now use to hone in on a particular aspect of classroom and/or school life. These tools include such teacher activities as collecting samples of students' work and assessing them over time; developing anecdotal records and time-samples of the activity of individual children, small groups, and whole classes; maintaining systematic daily journals; audio- and videotaping lessons to assess teacher-student interaction or teaching itself; and classroom and peer observations, surveys, questionnaires, and interviews.

We hold inquiry to be axiomatic to good teaching. Good teachers, like skilled actors, are constantly monitoring their audience, noting what brings attention, working to engage participants, and thinking ahead to create seamless transitions. But good teaching goes beyond stagecraft and moment-to-moment shifts in action and voice that will keep the audience alert. Good teaching is research. It is asking questions that help us to understand each of our students, questions that help us make the match between *what* we are teaching (content) with *who, where,* and *when* we are teaching (context). It is paying systematic attention to the outcomes of our instruction; determining what has been learned; figuring out what might work better; and refining, reshaping, and assessing our own work. It is also carefully attending to the consequences of policies that organize schooling and how they play out in the classroom.

Connecting Policy to Practice

As these studies show, inquiry in the hands of thoughtful teachers can illuminate practice—helping teachers to understand what works and what needs attention as well as to refine their craft. These studies have a particular relevance for teachers, school administrators, and policymakers whose focus is on public schools. In part this has to do with scale: for every documented case described here, there are hundreds, even thousands of teachers and students struggling with the same or similar issues. Thus, the studies speak to practicing teachers, helping them see ways of reading their classrooms and their schools and, perhaps, empowering them to do similar work and to enter into local and national discussions of education policy. In part, these studies speak to the unsettling fact that the majority of children in urban environments are being taught in underresourced public schools, and a disproportionate number of these children are living in poverty. How teachers who may have grown up and been educated in settings vastly different from those in which they are teaching learn to know their students, their students' families, and their students' communities; how they come to work in smart and caring ways that ensure the progress of their students—these are the stories that underlie this research and have fueled the entry of TNPI Fellows into the arena of education policy. We have come to understand that the success of any educational reform rests on the degree to which real teachers in real classrooms and schools can implement it. And we have come to realize that teacher research can inform understandings of education policy by showing how various initiatives fare in the everyday transactions of schooling. If they listen, policymakers can discern from these studies what obstacles must be overcome, and they can identify what issues must be addressed if all children are to succeed.

How We Do Action Research

Frances O'Connell Rust and Ellen Meyers

In the fall of 1998, we began our work together helping teachers learn how to do action research. Our intent then and now is to bring teachers' voices into the discussion of educational policy. We saw action research as a powerful vehicle for communicating to the larger public the complex, day-to-day realities of teachers and children in schools. Until then, teacher action research was something of a cottage industry in which teachers would focus on their own practice, sharing with close colleagues and making adjustments in their classrooms. Scholars like Marilyn Cochran-Smith and Susan Lytle (1993) wrote about teachers' research, but neither academicians nor teachers were engaging policymakers in teachers' work with the goal of bridging the gulf between classrooms and statehouses.

We began educating ourselves in the techniques of action research by reading Hubbard and Power's The Art of Classroom Inquiry *(1993). Four years later, the teachers in our network have developed a set of guidelines for conducting action research studies and disseminating their policy findings. What follows is their step-by-step guide for teachers interested in doing action research in their classrooms.* 🍎

The Question

Developing a good question is the essential first step in action research. Teachers are always asking questions about their work, but we found that it will take a month or two—if you have a support network where you can talk about your question and get challenging feedback—to hone in on the one question that you will follow over a year or more.

Typically, you start with "why" questions—"Why is there so much noise after lunch?"; yes-or-no questions—"Does attendance improve grades?"; "fix-it" questions—"What should I do when John refuses to read?"; or "how" questions that presume the efficacy of a particular intervention—"How does teaching students to use open-ended questions lead to higher order thinking?" These may not be the questions that you will ultimately explore; they may be too broad, too narrow, too superficial, or too presumptive. They may, however, give you some insight into what is of interest to you about your classroom and your teaching and help you get going.

We have found that good questions are free of educational jargon; they use simple, everyday words that make the point clear to all readers; and they do not prejudge the result. Examples of good questions include:

- What happens when students participate in the process of providing evidence of their understanding? (Wayne 2000)
- How much time is necessary for teachers to meet individual student needs and prepare students to achieve standards? (Peterson 2001)

Examples of good questions that need to be worded more clearly include:

- I began to wonder if my planning could be any better and if student achievement would increase if I planned my reading workshop with another colleague. Would our talk about all of our students help us to get a better handle on the strategies each child controlled, and the strategies they needed to refine in order to meet these standards? (Picard 2001)

    This question is very insightful, but it would be better stated in one clear sentence without jargon; for example, "Would planning with another colleague improve my students' reading skills?"
- To what extent would informal group and individual meetings with new teachers provide useful insights into their needs and concerns? (Fuller 2001)

This question deals with a key issue, but it presumes that the meetings will have an influence. A nonjudgmental question might ask, "What happens when an administrator meets with new teachers in informal group and individual meetings?"

Getting Started

One of the first activities that you can do is make a list of questions that you have about your classroom or your teaching or both. Try starting with "I wonder." You can always reframe your statements as questions. Choose one question on which you could spend some time. Ask yourself why this question is interesting to you, how you might go about answering it, and what might be the benefit to you of answering this question. If, after this conversation with yourself, you are still interested in the question, do a reality check by trying it out on a colleague.

Now it is time to shape your question as a research question. If framed properly, your question will help you determine what background reading you might need to do and which research tools to use. You will also need to describe the context of your study, discuss its importance, and refer to other research.

Permission

While you are probably asking questions about your practice daily, raising these questions as part of an action research project makes your thinking more public. If you are writing about your students and intend your study to go beyond you, you will need to change their names and to take steps to hide their identities. In most research, steps are taken to preserve the confidentiality of participants. However, as Zeni (2001) writes, "in the case of action research, the serious risks are generally those to privacy and reputation—risks that occur for the most part during the process of disseminating and publishing research." We have found it useful to begin by gaining permission. You should talk with the school principal and your students and communicate in writing with their parents. In some cases, you may need to get permission from your superintendent and school board. Your principal can be your guide here. We have also found that it is appropriate and helpful to share and celebrate your finished work with the participants.

Rationale

Your rationale describes the compelling reasons for conducting your study, and how the study is part of a bigger picture. Whether you are concerned about something as global as "community" in the school or new-teacher induction or something as personal and idiosyncratic as the design of your classroom, you want your reader to understand why this topic is important on a broader scale. Here are some examples from our teachers' studies:

It will come as no surprise that attending high school can be a pretty devastating experience. Instead of being in a place that promotes self-discovery and personal growth, it can be a place that fosters loneliness, humiliation, and failure. It can be a place that, in spite of the best intentions of its staff, fails to deal with the student as a whole person. Heavily focused on academic success, the staff never gets to know the young adult as an individual. They never get to know the myriad of personal problems or needs that their students bring to school. They are never really in a position to develop the full potential of their students because they simply do not know them well enough and to do more is beyond their present capabilities. As my research will show, there is a huge disconnect between students and staff. The consequences of this disconnect are enormous and the implications are far-reaching (Grashow 2001).

Over the next few years the New York City Board of Education predicts that thousands of teachers will be retiring. The result will almost certainly be that inexperienced, new teachers will staff many schools. This coincides with a movement toward higher standards and increased "high-stakes" standardized testing. Moreover, the shortage of qualified, experienced teachers is a nationwide problem. With large numbers of new teachers entering the system, we will need to compile a fund of knowledge about their needs and concerns in order to accommodate them better. The more we learn about integrating new teachers into the system, the better chance our children will have for a quality education (Fuller 2001).

My thoughts for this study were inspired by comparing the behavior and engagement of students within my classroom with the way those same children creatively used an open park for play. The comparison led me to wonder: Is there a connection between the environments of schools and student engagement? Do the learning spaces and their uses impact on student learning? If students feel more comfortable in a particular space, are they more engaged? Do they achieve more? (Kihn 2001)

Context

The comprehensiveness of your description is directly related to the focus of your question. If your study is part of a much larger study of an initiative in your school district, then it is important that you describe the district, even providing statistical information about it. However, if your study is essentially a self-study, an in-depth look at some aspect of your work with your students in your classroom, you do not need to do more than provide a general overview of the school and a good description of your class. This might include the number of students in your class, grade level, gender, and, if pertinent, such descriptors as languages spoken, socioeconomic level, and location—urban, suburban, or rural.

Relevant Research

This is also known as the "literature review." Reviewing current research on your topic is important because it situates your inquiry in the rich body of work that educators throughout the world have developed. It will also give you some fresh insights into the topic. We have found the Educational Research Information Center (ERIC) to be the most valuable tool for beginning the search: *www.askeric.org*. You can gain access to most educational journals in university libraries. Increasingly, these can also be found online.

You can refer to the studies in this book for ways in which classroom teachers have incorporated their library research into their studies. We cannot stress enough how crucial it is to do background work. Not only will it serve you well in your growth as a teacher researcher, it will also give you the authority to talk about your study and its relationship to educational policy.

Tools

Implicit in your question are the tools that you will use to answer that question. If you are just beginning to do action research, you will need to take some time to familiarize yourself with the various tools that are available to you. Some will be ones that you may already be using in your everyday work as a teacher, such as anecdotal records, notes from weekly reading conference, observations, or samples of student work. Developing new ways of looking at the classroom (collecting data) is fun and enlightening.

Here is a small sample of tools that our teachers have used:

• *Student, teacher, and parent surveys/questionnaires.* This is the first tool that everyone tries, but developing good questions is more difficult than you would think. You may want to start with a small trial survey that you test on a few students, colleagues, and/ or parents. This will help you refine your questions and figure out what you really want to know. For examples of surveys and questionnaires, see Chapter 5, Figures 5–3 and 5–4.

• *Interviews.* Interviewing takes practice. Interviews are personal, conducted one-on-one, and can take from a few minutes to an hour. Often, they are conducted with the aid of a tape recorder, and transcribing them takes time. Interviews can help you get beneath the surface of an issue, but doing an interview requires preparation and an awareness of certain pitfalls. You must learn not to ask leading questions, not to signal what it is that you want to hear, and how to control the interview so that it is productive. Because interviews are so time-consuming and can take an emotional toll, you will want to use them judiciously. You can read about interviews in Chapter 6 and see examples in the chapter Appendix B.

• *Notes from parent-teacher conferences.* To help parents feel comfortable, many teachers make notes immediately after conferences—while the experience is still fresh. These can be valuable data for your research, as you will see in Lara Goldstone's research in Chapter 4.

• *Student reading logs.* Reading logs are examples of student work. If truly authentic (the contents not prescribed), then you will find that logs are full of useful information about your students' writing and their thoughts about their reading

• *Field notes.* Field notes are your written observations of your students. You can take field notes in a variety of ways depending on what you are looking for. Matt Wayne, for example, used field notes at the beginning of his study just to find out about the reading habits of his students, which he discusses in Chapter 2. Others, like Natasha Warikoo, make notes after class by reflecting on lesson plans and interactions with students, which she discusses in Chapter 6.

• *Photographs.* Photographs are a great way to document work over time; for example, block building, classroom layout, or student art. You may not end up putting these into your final paper, but they can provide useful data.

• *Audio- and/or videotapes.* Audiotapes focus exclusively on talk and sound. As such, they can be useful if you are attending to teacher talk—your questioning, your interactions in small groups, and the amount of your talk relative to your students. Audiotapes are also useful for interviews. Video provides a wider perspective. You can get the benefits of an audiotape, plus a visual record of you and your students in action. In either case, you will need to think about why you are using this tool and how you will analyze the data that you gather. Ask a colleague to help you with this. Matt Wayne shows us a transcript of student conversation in Chapter 2, which you can find in his "Book Talk" appendix. Natasha Warikoo used videotaping in her math class and in a colleague's for her research. You can find a description of this in Chapter 6.

• *Email exchanges.* While none of the teachers whose work we have included in this book used email, email is likely to become part of your tool kit as computer use becomes more ubiquitous in schools. It could be used for documenting student-teacher and parent-teacher communication.

• *Anecdotal records.* Anecdotal records are used in case studies to document a particular set of behaviors of a child or a class. These are notes that provide a record of the time and the context of the behavior being studied as well as a full account of what happened. These are essential pieces of information for referrals, but can also be useful to help a teacher develop a better understanding of a particular child. See Lara Goldstone's case studies in Chapter 4 for a good use of anecdotal records.

• *Grades/report cards.* Your research can help you make the connection between your teaching and student achievement. If it is reflected in grades and on report cards, you will have made an accessible case for the instructional practice(s) that you are focusing on.

• *Attendance records.* Attendance records can provide interesting patterns, which, when correlated with other data such as student participation and handing in homework, may lead you to pay closer attention to certain students and design appropriate interventions.

• *Classroom maps.* Classroom maps are actual drawings of the classroom. These are essential for keeping track of how students are using the room, interacting with one another, and responding during class discussions. If classroom maps are used at the same time(s) over a period of days or weeks, they can be made into charts that reveal interesting patterns of the movement and/ or verbal flow in a classroom.

- *Peer observations.* To facilitate data collection using many of the tools we have described, you may want to turn to a colleague. You may also choose to observe your peers as part of your research. You can refer to Chapter 6 to learn how Natasha Warikoo used peer observations in her research.

- *Running records.* There is a specific protocol for running records that should be familiar to any teacher who is engaged in teaching reading. Running records help you to determine a student's reading skill and in what areas the reader is experiencing difficulty. Both Lara Goldstone and Matt Wayne make extensive use of running records in tracking student progress.

If you are new to action research, you should take some time to try various tools and become familiar with what information they can yield and how to make them part and parcel of your teaching. Working collaboratively with other teachers in a support network will help you to expand your repertoire and deepen your understanding of the power of a particular tool. You may also decide to expand your study beyond your own classroom by involving colleagues in designing, selecting, and implementing tools that will be used in their classrooms as well as yours. For example, teachers who have done research on lesson study have worked in this way.

Data

Data is the information generated by your research tools and takes many forms. Here are some examples:

- samples of student work collected over time, such as students' drawings, reading logs, writing samples, homework
- audio and video transcripts
- responses to questionnaires and surveys
- classroom maps that show movement and/or verbal flow
- notations from running records

- interview transcripts
- field notes taken over time
- photographs taken at various points during your study
- newspaper articles, newsletters, information bulletins, communiqués that relate to your study

If you use a tool such as student attendance records, you will have numerical data like the following: Student attendance for seminar during the spring shows that the average number of students absent from seminar over an eight-week period, by section, was 4.5 students in Section 1; 2.5 students in Section 2; 2.2 students in Section 3 (Tureski 2000).

If you use an open-ended questionnaire, you will have text that you will eventually need to code. Drawings can be data, as Diana Takenaga-Taga (2001) showed in her study of preservice teachers' perceptions of scientists. Try using charts, tables, and other graphic organizers to make your data clear. Think about describing your data in terms that make it easy to comprehend; for example, see Lisa Peterson's (2001) chart of the time she spent outside of school hours on school-related activities (Figure 1–1).

Always make sure to include a summary of your data in your paper. We have found that teachers new to action research often skip this step in their writing and go directly to analysis. Remember, your reader needs to know how you got there! You can even include samples of your data in appendixes.

Figure 1–1 Time Spent Outside of School Hours on School-Related Activities

WEEK OF FEBRUARY 19 (five days)		WEEK OF JUNE 4 (seven days)	
Planning/assessing	**8 hours**	Planning/assessing	**14.5 hrs**
Tutoring individuals	**7 hours**	Organizing 3-day class trip to Boston	**7-8 hours**
Extended day literacy program *(I am paid for work in this program.)*	**4 hours**	Preparing video for NY State permanent certification	**6 hours**
Organizing, preparing room	**4 hours**	Organizing, preparing room	**4 hours**

Analysis

Analysis is fun and messy. It always begins with your data. Try spreading out your data on your living room floor. Look at all you have collected. Begin simply by sorting according to the tools you used. Ask yourself what each tool is telling you about your question. For example, you may have samples of student work collected over time because you are focusing on some aspect of literacy skill development. Begin with the earliest samples. Describe them, focusing on the key attributes you are looking for. Move on to later samples. Again, focus on the key attributes. What has changed? Once you have done this, you need to think about how you can describe the changes. That becomes your analysis of that piece of data. But student work samples may be only one of the tools you used to pursue your question. If test scores are another, then you will need to look at early and late scores and compare them. Again, you will focus on the key attributes you are using to guide your inquiry and then determine change. As you continue in this way with your various data sources, you should ask yourself about the best ways to describe the changes you notice.

Here are some techniques for beginning to organize your data:

- Code your transcripts.
- Sort your annotated field notes around various topics.
- Collate the data from your questionnaires and surveys.
- Make a time line with your photographs.

Your choice about how to organize your data and what technique(s) to employ will depend on your data and what you are looking for. If this process is new to you, you will need to find a reference on qualitative research or seek out a colleague who has expertise in this arena. In the Teachers Network Policy Institute, we spend time each month helping one another examine data and learn techniques for organizing and analyzing it.

Once you have combed through your various data sources and analyzed them, you are ready to make your case. Think of your

Figure 1–2 Analysis of Study Group Conversation (Arnold 2002)

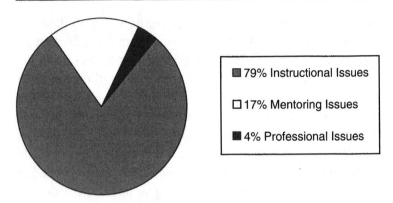

analysis as akin to a legal brief: you are gathering the data and organizing it in ways that support the argument you will make in your conclusion.

Here are a couple of techniques for presenting your analysis:

• Case study of a student, small group, or classroom. The case study format enables you to bring your various data sources together. Penny Arnold (2002) did this in her study of teachers working as mentors with student teachers. She used a pie chart to focus on what they talked about (see Figure 1–2).

• Telling a story. You might begin your write-up with a story that emerges from your classroom and that illustrates or contains the various elements of the study you have just completed. While the story is your lead, the shape of your study may follow the conventional outline we are following in this chapter. Diana Takenaga-Taga began her study of preservice teachers' views of scientists at work with the following story:

> In the fall of 1999, I asked my science preservice students, "How many of you had science instruction in elementary school?" Very few hands went up leading me to believe that the majority of my undergraduate students had poor science education back-

grounds. After some discussion, I learned that my students had science phobias and were apprehensive about the class they were sitting in. Science was viewed as a negative, "difficult" subject only to be understood by few individuals. If science had a portrait, it would look like a Caucasian man who wore a white coat and worked in a laboratory surrounded by test tubes, bottles, and books (Takenaga-Taga 2001).

Conclusions and Policy Implications

Your conclusion emerges from your analysis. It tells the reader what you learned. It may also point to further areas for study. Chris Mullin's and Jerry Swanitz' (1999) study of professional development around computer use provides a good example. They asked two questions:

1. Will training teachers in the use of problem- and project-based learning, including student use of Internet resources, increase the degree to which teachers use technology as an instructional tool?
2. Over time, will teacher implementation of problem-based, technology-rich lesson plans lead to improved student learning?

At the end of their study, they concluded, "Our study indicates that teacher use of technology increases with proficiency but, more importantly, with knowledge of how to actually construct powerful learning activities in which students have hands-on use of technology."

Their conclusion makes sense in light of the analysis that precedes it and leads well into their policy recommendations:

- Technology implementation plans should allot at least 15 percent of the budget to provide staff development. Clearly, spending the entire budget on hardware and software will yield little in the way of sound educational results.
- Technology grants should not only require that a percentage of the budget be set aside for staff development, but there

should be a stipulation that staff development include instruction and practice on how to incorporate student use of technology into learning activities.

As this example demonstrates, policy implications should connect with your data presentation, analysis, and conclusions. When you write your policy recommendations, it is important to be specific. Include concrete actions that policymakers can take. Be specific about which policymakers can implement your recommendations. Sarah Picard's (2001) policy recommendations are a good example. In response to her question, "Would planning with another colleague improve my students' reading skills?" and based on her data, analysis, and conclusions, she presents the following policy recommendations:

1. At the district level, structures should be developed that provide for collaborative teaching during the school day.
2. At the contractual level, teachers should have the option to work an extended day to allow for collaborative planning.
3. At the school level, principals and teachers should work together to create conditions that encourage collaborative relationships around instruction.

Last Words and Next Steps

Action research is hard work. We have learned that doing good research, like learning to teach well, takes time. Your first study may be tough going, but we promise you that if you stick with it and network with other teacher researchers, you will get better at it. Action research is most successful when teachers have figured out how to bring it into their everyday teaching—no small task, but well worth the effort. Examining what you do every day in a systematic way makes you a better teacher.

A great way to get a sense of the power of inquiring in this way about your teaching is to read the studies that we have included in this book. We also encourage you to go to our website *www.teachersnetwork.org/tnpi* and watch our action research

14

Figure 1–3 Action Research Paper Review Criteria Form

Action Research Paper Review Criteria

Name:

Section	Comments
Question • Clear and simple • No prejudgment	
Rationale for Study • Clear and simple • Broad scale reasons • Bigger picture?	
Background/Context • Basic facts • Statistics	
Research • Relevance • New insights/trends • No editorializing	
Tools • Research methods • Clarity • Appropriateness	
Data • Different forms • Numerical or factual • Summary • Clear and thoughtful presentation • Relevance	
Analysis • Connection to data • Explanations • Make a case • Clear	
Policy Recommendations • Reflects learning • Clear and targeted • Connection with study	

video, which features Matt Wayne and his students conducting research in their classroom.

When you have completed your study, we suggest that you use the Action Research Paper Review Criteria form that we have included here (Figure 1–3) to make sure that you have all the essential elements of a study. This will help you to know that it is ready for dissemination and publication. Email it to us at *info@teachersnetwork.org* and we'll put it on our website!

2

Our Unfinished Story
Rising to the Challenge of
High Standards

Matt Wayne

Matt Wayne began his research by asking, "How can we get the right books into the hands of struggling readers so that they get excited about reading and attain the challenging reading standards?" The story he tells brings to light some of the inadequacies of school budgeting and the problems of bypassing teachers in decisions about classroom materials.

Wayne began by identifying his struggling readers through test scores, surveys, and running records. He then developed a number of interventions, the success of which he assessed through observations, audiotapes, and case studies. By the time his research was complete, a majority of the students' percentiles on the statewide reading tests increased, in some cases, significantly. 🍎

The Unfinished Story

"Great job, Yolanda! Now let's talk about what you just read. What did *you* think about it?" I sat back on the couch in our reading area to listen to Yolanda explain her thoughts on what she had just read to me. It was the first week of school, and I was conferring with the students to get an idea of their attitudes toward reading and to assess their reading levels. Yolanda did not sound confident as she shared her thoughts. "Well, um, I don't like how this one guy did that to the other guy. I mean, I don't know. I guess it was okay, but I'm not sure." I encouraged her to trust her thoughts; she shouldn't worry about giving me a "wrong" answer. She meekly shared a bit more. Then I asked her what she thought of the book. She replied, "It's okay, but I don't really like to read." Warning bells went off in my head.

Still thinking how I could help Yolanda learn to enjoy reading, I went on to talk to Tyrone. He was reluctant to read aloud to me and obviously uncomfortable with his reading skills. While several students in the class were confident readers and eager to share their ideas, most did not believe they were capable readers nor did they think others would value their ideas about what they read. Yolanda and Tyrone expressed an attitude toward reading that was prevalent in my sixth-grade classroom.

Framing the Question

In the midst of the recent talk in this country of high standards for all students, it is easy to forget Yolanda's apprehensions and Tyrone's insecurities and what reaching standards means to them. According to public opinion polls, Americans are in favor of high academic standards for children. Public Agenda, a non-profit polling group, discovered that 71 percent of Americans say that with higher standards the education of our nation's students will improve. Ninety percent of the public—parents, teachers, business and political leaders—do not believe students are under too much academic pressure. A whopping 92 percent are in favor of teaching basics such as reading, writing, and arithmetic to a high standard (Johnson and Duffett, 1-5). Rarely is such support found for an education initiative. Then again, who is not going to be in favor of high standards?

The real question becomes *how* can we help students reach high standards? This challenge is what drives the inquiry and policy recommendations presented here. I am investigating ways in which a New York City middle school teacher can help struggling sixth-grade students achieve the New Standards adopted by the city—specifically, the Reading Standards component of the English Language Arts Middle School Standards. I have spent this school year exploring this broad question. I have not found any definitive answers. However, I believe my research tells an important story about the ways in which thoughtfulness and caring can be brought to a school on a consistent basis and how such an atmosphere affects learning and achievement. This is, in fact, Yolanda's and Tyrone's story—as well as that of all the other students in our class who are working so hard to be successful readers and learners.

The Setting: New Standards in Schools

As I begin to explain my research, it is important to understand the larger context of my efforts. New Standards, which have been adopted by my district and school, were established in 1991 as part of a collaboration between the Learning Research and Development Center at the University of Pittsburgh and the National Center on Education and the Economy in partnership with states and urban school districts. In 1983, a comprehensive review of the state of education in the United States was published. During the decade following this report, titled *A Nation at Risk,* there was a sense of urgency regarding the performance of public schools. Educators, business leaders, politicians, and universities were all continually searching for ways to offer children a "world class education," improve children's "higher order thinking skills and problem-solving abilities," and prepare them to be "democratic citizens"—as the 1983 report demands (National Commission on Excellence in Education 1983, 3). Lauren Resnick, one of the founders of New Standards, noted in 1987, "The question of whether schools can do a better job of teaching American children 'higher order thinking skills' [and offer a world-class education] is very much in the air. It arises in Congressional hearings ... and it is reflected in public concern that changing demands are not being met, students' preparation for college is less than satisfactory, and general problem-solving abilities remain low." (1) Resnick and others addressed these questions by beginning the New Standards project (Resnick and Resnick 1989). Their basic premise is that intelligence is not innate and all students, given the appropriate support and surroundings, will in time achieve standards. From this idea comes the notion of effort-based learning.

The New Standards Commission worked on creating performance-based standards that would reflect such effort and describe for the major content areas "what students should know and be able to do and how good is good enough" (New York City Board of Education 1997, 3). Educators from around the country and many professional organizations—such as the National Council of Teachers of English and the National Council of Teachers of Mathematics—contributed to the development and publication of New Standards.

In 1997, the first national New Standards document was published. It outlined performance standards in English language arts, mathematics, and science at the elementary, middle, and high school levels. The document not only includes detailed descriptions of each performance assessment standard, but numerous samples of real student work that reflect standards work. By this time, the Chancellor of the New York City Public Schools and the New York City Board of Education had placed their support behind New Standards. They commissioned teachers, supervisors, and administrators representing all districts and superintendents to customize the collection of student work samples contained in the New York City edition so that the document would be relevant to the practice of New York City teachers. This work was ready for the 1998 school year and disseminated to all New York City teachers. In addition, the English Language Arts Performance (ELAP) test replaced the California Test of Basic Reading Skills (CTB) for fourth and eighth graders. The ELAP test is based on the New Standards work. This New Standards work guides my classroom practice and professional development in the school and the district.

The Reading Standards

A complaint often heard after *A Nation at Risk* was that education was not providing clear outcomes for students. The New

Standards document responded to this critique by offering thorough educational outcomes for elementary, middle, and high school students. With respect to English language arts, the New Standards document has five specific standards: (1) Reading; (2) Writing; (3) Speaking, Listening, and Viewing; (4) Conventions, Grammar, and Usage of the English Language; and (5) Literature. For each standard, there are further requirements that the students must fulfill.

I have chosen to focus on the reading standards for two reasons. First, reading is an essential aspect of becoming a lifelong learner. If I hope to inspire an enthusiasm for learning, then encouraging students' interest in reading must be an integral part of my practice. Second, at this moment in education, teaching students to read is one of the nation's foremost concerns. It is a priority in most public documents concerning the education of our children: from Goals 2000 on the national level, to initiatives passed in California and the *Compact for Learning* in New York on the state level, to the chancellor's mandates for New York City Public Schools and districts' literacy initiatives on the local level.

During the course of a year, students are expected to read at least twenty-five books by different authors and from different genres. In addition, they must read a wide variety of other types of texts, such as informational material or public documents. The students are also expected to produce evidence of reading that addresses the full complexities of the texts read. Finally, the reading standards demand a certain "quality and complexity of the material" appropriate to the middle school reading level.

The New Standards document does not specify how students are to reach these goals. That was not its intent. The middle school reading standards are a destination, a place for students to reach by the end of the eighth grade. The journey there is the challenge for teachers. The venture becomes more earnest when many of the students in the class are struggling with reading and enter the class far below standard. It is at this juncture that my personal research of my classroom began.

Our School

I work in Manhattan at a small middle school of 175 students that is beginning its third full year. The school is housed in and grew out of an elementary school near Chinatown. The population is roughly one-third Chinese, one-third African American, and one-third Hispanic. Most of the students come from the nearby public housing apartments and qualify for free lunch. The school is an inclusion school, which means that special education students are in the regular classroom. I have a sixth-grade class of twenty-five students, two of whom are designated special education and five others who receive resource room services. In our school, the language arts teachers move up the grades with their students, so my sixth-grade class will be with me for language arts through the eighth grade.

Researching the Classroom

My research has taken two forms. I have been and continue to be a "teacher-researcher" in my classroom, as well as a researcher of the professional literature concerning the teaching of reading. I am modeling my research efforts on the action research method discussed by Emily F. Calhoun in her book *How to Use Action Research in the Self-Renewing School* and *The Art of Classroom Inquiry* by Hubbard and Power (1993). Calhoun defines action research as, "a way of saying, 'Let's study what's happening at our school [and in our classroom] and decide how to make it a better place'" (Calhoun 1994, 19). To do this, she organizes the process of action research into a continuous cycle of five steps: (1) select area of study, (2) collect data, (3) organize data, (4) analyze and interpret data, and (5) take action. She notes that action research is not intended to evolve so neatly in the school or the classroom. New data might cause a rethinking of the area of study that can then lead to different analyses, other actions being taken, and so forth. She organizes these steps as a spiral, each one pushing the other forward and then coming back in on itself (3). This spiraling process took effect as I questioned my own assumptions and challenged my own practices. Hubbard and Powers provide a variety of strategies for teacher research. I drew extensively on these.

I also began a more personal and thorough examination of the students' reading habits and their attitudes toward reading. I did a short survey of the students to learn more about their experiences with reading. In addition, I began taking running records of the students' reading. A running record consists of teacher notes about errors or miscues made as a student reads aloud a passage from a text. The student is not expected to read the text cold and is given the context of the passage. Besides the test scores, the survey, and the running record, I am, of course, always assessing the students through observation and classroom interaction.

Having collected data on my students' reading, I decided to focus my action research question on what and how many books they chose to read. Cunningham and Stanovich (1998) argue that reading has significant cognitive consequences and that the amount of reading students do affects the development of these cognitive abilities and predicts whether students will become avid readers or not. They maintain that "we see that very early in the reading process poor readers who experience greater difficulty in breaking the spelling-to-sound code, begin to be exposed to much less text than their more skilled peers" (8). For the more advanced reader, "the sheer volume of reading done by the better reader has the potential to provide many advantages [in their future reading and cognitive development]" (8). Cunningham and Stanovich found that as struggling readers fall farther behind their peers who read well, they are given *fewer* texts to read, not more. This downward spiral continues until struggling readers barely have any opportunity to be successful readers. They point out that "students who get off to a fast start in reading are more likely to read more over the years" (14). They conclude by making their claim for the importance of volume with respect to reading ability and for cognitive ability.

From CTB Reading scores, I found that I had seven "struggling readers" in the class. These are students who score below the twenty-fifth percentile and who are considered by the district to be "at-risk." Coupled with my research on reading, this data led me to ask, "How can we get books into the hands of struggling readers so that they become excited about reading and attaining the challenging reading standards?"

Getting Started

My initial observations took place during the first weeks of September and were focused on student choice of books to read independently. I observed their selections from our classroom library, which has a fair variety of books on many different levels. I observed that Lupe, one of my struggling readers, was choosing books that were on the fourth- or fifth-grade level, books that her friends were also reading. This surprised me because during our first running record, she had difficulty with a text from a second-grade book. From the manner in which she was turning the pages, I could tell immediately that Lupe did not understand what she was reading. My suspicions were confirmed when I sat down on the rug in our reading area to confer with her about the book. Although we talked as a class about strategies for choosing a book, my observations of Lupe's book choice and that of other students proved to me that our talk was not helping the students make good book choices. My efforts as a teacher-researcher were making it clear that middle school students do not want to be seen reading "baby books" when they see their friends choosing longer, more difficult books. The struggling readers in my class needed help in choosing appropriate books to read.

At the same time, I was taking field notes on students' reading habits. In our class, students have independent reading time from 9:35 to 9:55 A.M. During that time, the students read independently while I have individual conferences. I decided to do a spot check of the students' reading habits three times during the twenty minutes. I gave them five minutes to settle down and then noted what students were doing at 9:40 A.M. I repeated this process at 9:50 A.M. and 9:55 A.M. I noted my spot checks down on a chart. I performed these spot checks over three class periods. The results of these spot checks revealed that some children were consistently off-task and others had difficulty getting on-task. At 9:40 A.M. most were still not actively engaged in reading. Some looked at their books while others did not even have books out. These students needed strategies to help them use their independent reading time more productively.

Taking Action

With this thought in mind and intrigued with my initial data, my priority now was to increase opportunities for the struggling readers to read more and to successfully interact with text. To best do this, the action I took was to reorganize our classroom library. Following the suggestion of a literacy support person from the district's professional development team, I organized the library books by reading level, creating four different categories. Inside each book I placed a colored sticker: red indicating the easiest level, blue the next easiest, then yellow, then green. To determine book levels, I looked at general characteristics—length, print size, illustration, vocabulary, and syntax. I then put two stickers into each student's reading journal. The stickers indicated which color-coded section the students were to choose their books from. By sending them to a particular section, I sought to increase the chance that they would pick books on their level while still having the freedom to choose books within each section.

Presenting the new library system to the class was a concern. I knew it would be fairly obvious that some colors represented easier books. When explaining the new library system, I picked up some of my "top choices," telling them a little about each book and why I liked it. I made sure to recommend a lot of the red (easier) books and gave every student at least one red or blue sticker, hoping to demonstrate that everyone goes to all sections. Friends could still choose the same books, but this time struggling readers wouldn't be lost. And those more skilled readers still had one sticker that would give them a more challenging choice.

To determine which books the students were checking out I introduced a sign-out sheet. By November, I discovered that all students in the class were choosing more appropriate books, and the volume of books being read even by struggling readers increased to the point where more books were needed.

New York City teachers receive $200 to spend as "Teacher's Choice" money. I used the entire amount to buy new books for the classroom with an amazingly positive result. When I brought in the new books—readable stories of high interest—I literally had to curb the students' enthusiasm.

The Story Spirals On

Having students read books at their level is a necessary first step if they are expected to graduate to the first standard of reading twenty-five books of the appropriate "quality and complexity" by the end of middle school. Standards also require students to "demonstrate" reading skills. An example of evidence that demonstrates "at standard" reading skills is "a literary response paper [or] a research report [in which the student] makes and supports warranted and responsible assertions about the texts; supports assertions with elaborated and convincing evidence; draws the text together to compare and contrast themes; makes perceptive and well-developed connections; evaluates writing strategies and elements of the author's craft" (New York City Board of Education 1997, 92). The reading standards require written evidence, and the ELAP tests require written explanations of the students' thoughts on readings. With this knowledge in mind, I began to research how my class showed evidence of their reading skills.

In addition to reading conferences and spot checks, I also require that students maintain a journal to record a brief retelling of the reading and then a page of thoughts, opinions, and reactions to the readings. This is an effective way to know if the students are both understanding their reading and reflecting as they read.

I found that a page of thoughts, opinions, and reactions was a struggle for many of my sixth graders, especially those who were having difficulty reading. It is one thing for the students to be finally reading books that they understand; it is quite another for them to articulate in writing what happens in the story and their thoughts on it.

We spent several months working in the journals. There was much good conversation around our reading during our whole-group read-alouds, small-group reading activities, and individual conferences. Unfortunately, these discussions did not consistently translate into successful journal entries.

By late November, it was important for me to find ways to get the students writing their thoughts and analyses of their reading. I distributed a survey in which I asked them for their opinions regarding the reading logs. Their responses were overwhelmingly negative. Apparently, having to write three times a week was diminishing the very joy of reading I had tried so hard to encourage since September. This valuable insight spurred me to take some immediate corrective action.

As previously mentioned, students were talking a lot about the reading done in class. Some children who were not writing even a single paragraph in their reading journals were speaking volumes about what they were reading in class. However, I had yet to offer any formal opportunities for them to talk about their in-class and at-home independent reading experiences. I decided to make book talks about their independent reading an integral part of the English language arts class. The students met every other day with a book-talk partner to participate in a discussion about their reading selections. During the talks, which lasted twenty minutes, the students would retell what happened in the reading, react to it, discuss reading strategies we practiced in class, and ask each other questions. I had the students write advertisements about themselves so they could choose compatible reading partners.

The first book talk was, for me, one of the most exciting moments of the year. It occurred shortly after I brought in the new books for our library. The room was abuzz with excitement. I sat in on several groups' conversations and was extremely impressed with what I heard.

I wanted to more thoroughly investigate the students' conversations, so while I was in the classroom monitoring and listening in on some of the book talks, I sent two pairs of students to the school library to tape their conversations. After each taping I would listen to the students' book talks and assess their work. While many of the students in the class had difficulty expressing their ideas about their reading in writing, most were able to clearly articulate their thoughts about their reading during the book-talk conversations. A transcript of Tyrone's book talk with his reading partner, Newman, offers an excellent example of this (see the appendix at the end of this chapter). During his book talk, Tyrone retells what he has read and shows obvious enthusiasm for the story. I was most impressed by his ability to analyze the characters and support his analysis with examples from the text. This is something we had worked on for a long time, yet this was the first real demonstration I had that Tyrone was doing such a thing in his own reading life.

Listening to the tapes of other students confirmed that they, too, had interesting ideas about their reading, although they had been unable to express them in writing. I found this encouraging and did not give up on the writing aspect of the students' responses, but scaled back the frequency of the journal writing. I also repeatedly reminded them that their reading journal entries should be as informative as their book talks. I hoped that the juxtaposition of book talks and writing would help to make the reading journals an easier task.

From Classroom Research
to Collaborative Reflection

While the book talks were extremely successful, there were still students who were not showing the kind of skill development that the New Standards requires. Yolanda presented me with one of my most difficult challenges. Both her book talks and her writing were minimal. Even though her book-talk partner was a close friend, she had a difficult time communicating anything about the reading. Invariably, the discussion resulted either in her partner's talking the whole time or in Yolanda's changing the subject, which distracted both girls.

I realized that further reflection was necessary if I were going to succeed at encouraging Yolanda to even start down the path of successfully completing the middle school reading standards. Due to our status as a special education inclusion elementary and middle school, our school was awarded a Least Restrictive Environment (LRE) grant. Our principal was given broad discretion to use this money toward any activity that would help create the "least restrictive environment" in the school. The middle school has many new staff members, and the principal determined it would be advantageous to use the money to fund weekly meetings where we could share our ideas about the school, the students, and our practice. Although she led the first few meetings, she wanted the teachers to take turns as facilitators. I viewed this as an excellent opportunity to discuss my classroom research and the challenges Yolanda presented.

I brought my field notes to the meeting as well as my anecdotal evidence and some of Yolanda's work so that we could develop a case study. Her history, science, and math teachers had all experienced similar resistance from Yolanda in their classes. Other teachers were able to relate Yolanda's struggles to those of students in their own classes. The meeting evolved into a brainstorming session in which we discussed teaching strategies to address the needs of students like Yolanda. We all left the session encouraged to try the shared strategies in our own classrooms. For example, one teacher shared her success with Yolanda when she had her use the computer to write an assignment.

I, too, had excellent results when I encouraged Yolanda to do her reading journals on the computer. She started to come up during study hall and lunch to finish her writing. I also used this strategy with several other students, and their work and work habits slowly improved. As the staff continued to come together to share case studies from our classes, I discovered further strategies to try out to help my struggling readers work toward meeting the reading standards.

Building Collaboration

The case studies offered us an opportunity to share our professional expertise, explore ideas that were immediately relevant to our own practice, and learn about each other's teaching methods and struggles in the classroom. I surveyed the teachers after several meetings that revolved around case studies to obtain their opinion of the exercise. Seven out of the eight teachers who responded to the survey judged the case studies to be "helpful" or "very helpful." Six of the eight found these meetings "more valuable" than previous group meetings in which the conversations revolved more around administrative and discipline issues and philosophical questions about the direction of the school. One teacher wrote about how discussing the case studies helped her implement new writing strategies. Another teacher noted that she was able to utilize suggestions that came out of the discussions for a number of students who demonstrated similar difficulties. Most teachers surveyed want to continue case studies next year and believe that they could be done in an even better way if a more structured system to follow up on the students were in place. I suspect that being able to talk about specific students and share ideas and strategies relevant to our daily classroom lives sparked the positive response to the case studies.

Student Outcomes

Four times during the course of the year, our school administers Reading Progress Indicator tests. These tests are used to help students prepare for the statewide reading tests. The tests become increasingly more difficult so as to reflect the progress the students should be making over the course of a year.

To determine my students' progress, I compared the scores on the first two tests to the scores on the final two tests. According to the Reading Progress Indicator, our class as a whole registered a 3 percent increase in scores over the year. More impressive, only one student's score decreased by a significant factor (over 8 percent, or more than four questions on the exam), while eleven students' scores improved by a significant factor. My struggling readers did improve slightly (2 percent overall), yet their scores did not reflect a significant improvement.

I also received positive results from the statewide reading test (CTB). This is a multiple-choice test and the students' raw scores are compared with those of students across the state and the nation to find a national percentile. It is this percentile that affects the students' chances to be promoted and to be admitted to a high school. The percentile is also used as a criterion for judging the performance of the school. However, the CTB did not include written questions about readings like the ones on the New Standards exam (the ELAP) that all students began taking in 2001.

The results of the CTB test were similar to that of the Reading Progress Indicators. While our class has a long way to go to improve compared to the rest of the nation, I was encouraged by the fact that a majority of students' percentiles did improve. It is also interesting to note that our class average of 40.6 percent was the highest average among the fifth-, sixth-, and seventh-grade classes in our school.

Analysis of Reading Progress Indicator Scores
one student showed a significant decrease (8% or more)
seven students showed a small decrease (less than 8%)

five students showed a small increase (less than 8%)
eleven students showed a significant increase (8% or more)

Analysis of Statewide Reading Test (CTB)
three students showed a significant decrease (8% or more)
seven students showed a small decrease (less than 8%)
six students showed a small increase (less than 8%)
seven students showed a significant increase (8% or more)
one Limited English Proficient student was exempt

Our Unfinished Story

Now that students are reading books at an appropriate level, the number of available new titles in our classroom is rapidly diminishing. Yolanda has read all of our adapted classics, and Tyrone is through the entire Time Warp Trio series. Knowing that the students need to keep reading through June and beyond, we went to the children's library at New York City's main branch to discover new titles. As the librarian began speaking to the class, she asked the students if they liked to read. I held my breath as I waited for their response. To my immense personal and professional satisfaction, the entire class raised their hands and a chorus of "yes!" rang out. In addition to my research, reflection, and collaboration, knowing that the hard work of all the students in the class has led to their improved attitudes toward reading encourages me to work even harder to help all students reach high standards. I look forward to working with the staff to make my policy recommendations a part of the school culture and discovering what other stories surface in our quest to meet high standards and develop a lifelong appreciation for learning.

From Research to Policy Recommendations

No policy can take into account the individual needs of every student. However, I believe we can use education policy to create an environment that expressly allows teachers, principals,

Figure 2–1 Mosaic of Increased Student Achievement Through Collective Improvement

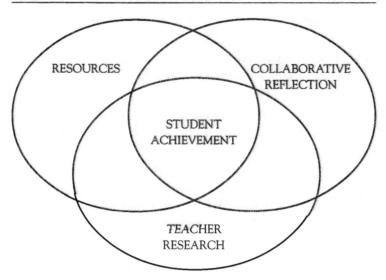

and school administrators to consider the needs of students. My recommendations call for educators to wisely invest time, energy, and resources into the day-to-day work of education. The mosaic in Figure 2–1 offers an understanding of how I believe an improvement in teacher research, collaborative reflection, and education resources can collectively lead to increased student achievement.

I propose that schools

- provide teachers with the professional development, support, and tools to do classroom research;
- schedule regular meetings among teacher-researchers during which teachers are responsible for sharing their classroom research, reflecting on classroom practice, and following up on the conversations that take place during these meetings; and
- allow teachers to decide what resources to purchase for their classrooms.

Teachers as Researchers

The process of investigating the classroom has been instrumental in helping my students work toward attaining the reading standards. If classroom research were to become a part of the school environment, teachers would have a systematic way to investigate their own teaching and their students' learning. Based on my experience in the Teachers Network Policy Institute, I recommend that schools introduce classroom research as a schoolwide policy at the beginning of the school year. More than likely, there are already teachers in the school or district who practice classroom research, whether they explicitly call it that or not. These teachers can share the benefits of this practice. Also, I recommend that teachers be given appropriate materials like this book so that they can become familiar with the practice.

Next, I would encourage teachers to pursue any question that might be of interest to them. Such openness is necessary if teacher-research is going to succeed as a policy initiative. It would be a grave mistake for a school or a district to mandate what must be researched. If teachers are not invested in their research then the strategy will not be put into use in the classroom.

After the first few weeks of school, I encourage teachers to share their questions and initial forays into research in an open, nonthreatening forum. Support and encouragement can take various forms such as classroom observations, conversations among colleagues about action research, and administrative recognition of research that has positively affected student achievement or teacher practice. Providing the tools for action research might mean helping teachers learn various ways of making fieldnotes, developing surveys that might help teachers learn more about their students, making tape recorders available so teachers can audiotape their lessons or student conversations, and even videotaping teachers so they can actually see their teaching and use it for self-study.

Collaborative Reflection

Having laid the foundation for teacher-research as a part of the school culture, my second policy recommendation is to introduce collaborative reflection to the school community. Without a forum in which to share their classroom research, teacher-researchers limit the success of their inquiries.

At our school we have a scheduled common preparatory period for teachers to plan and meet together. This common preparatory period occurs when the students are either in gym or an elective class. The primary lesson I learned from my experience is that if a school makes common preparatory time a priority, then the schedule will be organized to make it happen. Follow-up to these meetings is critical. Formalized reflection tools such as the charts that appear in Figures 2–2 and 2–3 might encourage such follow-up.

The first chart I created (Figure 2–2) simply has two columns and works like a double-entry journal often used in English language arts classes. As a teacher shares his classroom inquiry, a participant at the meeting records the teacher's research and tools in the left column. The ideas resulting from the teacher's class research and practice are recorded in the right column. This simple and effective way of documenting the research work of the teachers can be continually referred to as a resource by other teachers who have the same students or who are interested in doing the same type of research in their own classrooms. Instead of the teachers' research and resulting conversations being just more great ideas that join the ether of ideas floating around the building, they become a concrete record of the work being done in the school.

The second chart (Figure 2–3) offers an opportunity to explore the results of teacher research and collaborative discussion with a bit more depth. The case study or classroom situation being discussed at the meeting is briefly documented in the first column. In the second column, the strategies that are recommended in the course of the meeting are noted. The third

35

Figure 2–2 Collaborative Reflection Chart 1

Collaborative Reflection:
Accountable Follow-Up
(Chart 1)

Tools and Research	Reflection and Strategies
Field notes of students during independent reading time. Used a chart to mark the activity of students at certain times.	• Students need to choose books which interest them more. • Students need to focus on getting right to reading * Lesson on choosing books * Time students when they are preparing to read.

column is to be filled at the next meeting or after a few meetings. This column documents efforts to implement the strategies being discussed as well as their success or failure. A final column might be added to note how this work has affected the student's progress in meeting the New Standards. Such charts serve as excellent resources for teachers who want to see which strategies are successful in which situations. While all students are

Figure 2–3 Collaborative Reflection Chart 2

Collaborative Reflection:
Accountable Follow-Up
(Chart 2)

Case Study/ Classroom Situation	Strategies	Follow–Up	Progress Toward Standards
Yolanda—unmotivated reader and writer. Not working well in reading journal.	• Use creative projects to encourage her to respond to her reading • Allow her to use computer to write her journal entries	• Yolanda did not do an art project to respond to her reading • Started writing a lot on the computer. Also more motivated in class. Her change was noted by other teachers	Producing written work. Needs to expand ideas to meet standard E1b

different, certain "tricks of the trade" can be applied in a variety of settings.

Such a record could prove invaluable to teachers who are trying to help their kids reach standards. I suggest keeping notes in a big binder marked "Collaborative Research" and displaying it prominently in the teachers' meeting room, to make it accessible to any colleague with an interest in knowing about the teacher-research and reflection being done in the school.

Resources

My final policy recommendation is that schools give teachers discretion over funds for buying classroom resources. Teachers are in the best position to address the needs of their students. My own practice in the classroom has given me an excellent understanding of where my students are in terms of reading and what types of literature might engage them the most. I also have a good idea of which supplementary materials help them produce evidence of having met the standard.

This recommendation is grounded in current research on school reform and in research on the professional development of teachers. Linda Darling-Hammond maintains that, "although things like standards, funding, and management are essential supports, the sine qua non of education is whether teachers know how to make complex subjects accessible to diverse learners and whether they can work in partnership with parents and other educators to support children's development" (Darling-Hammond 1997a, 297). She goes on to outline what teachers need to know and be able to do, and then discusses the subject of curriculum resources and technologies. She states that "teachers need to be able to connect their students with sources of information and knowledge . . . that allow for the exploration of ideas [and] the acquisition and synthesis of information" (Darling-Hammond 1997a, 327). For this to happen "new approaches [to teaching] redesign the work and responsibilities of all teachers so that they have opportunities to engage in decision making, knowledge production, peer coaching, and continual redesign of teaching and schooling" (Darling-Hammond 1997a, 328).

At our school, the principal and teachers agree that the teachers are in the best position to select appropriate resources for their students. During our spring professional development day, we discussed which books and resources to order for the coming year. The principal explained how much money was available and how to order materials. We did not have to decide immediately which materials to order; we had time to explore what might best meet the needs of our students. The principal invited district experts to meet with us so that we would be aware of the wide array of resources available in order to make informed decisions.

These three policy recommendations—researching our students, reflecting together, and searching for the appropriate resources—will help create an environment that makes it possible for *all* students to meet the challenge of high standards. Taken together, they offer schools an opportunity to use time, energy, and resources in ways that can create the thoughtfulness and caring needed among teachers to help all students reach standards.

Appendix: Book Talk

On January 21, 1999, Tyrone and Newman held a book talk that they taped. In the beginning of the conversation they retold *Doug's Vampire Caper* (Krulik 1997), the story they both had read. The transcript picks up where they begin to share their thoughts on the book. They are making text-to-self connections, a reading strategy we had been practicing in class. Note how they support their ideas with examples from the text and actually listen to each other and respond to their partner's ideas.

Tyrone: Are you . . . are you ready now, Newman?

Newman: Yes, Tyrone, I'm ready. You go first; you do your text-to-self.

Tyrone: Uh, I agree on the kids thinking that Skeeter was the vampire. 'Cause Skeeter's like a lonely kid and he doesn't have any brothers or sisters or nothing. And he always stays down in the basement by himself. So, it's like, vampires like dark spaces and sleep upside down where nobody can see them. And so Skeeter, he really . . . he really loves being in his room in the basement so it's dark and damp and nobody comes down there a lot. Except for Doug 'cause Doug comes to play with him. So . . . then . . . I think that they were right about accusing him, but I'm not sure about Doug 'cause Doug knows that Skeeter's his best friend. And, but Doug still goes with the gang. Of course

Doug is going to listen to the kids that don't really like him. They don't really like him, they just . . . they just like to send him doing crazy things and stuff to get him in trouble. Newman's gonna take it away.

Newman: At first, in the beginning of the story, I always thought it was Connie because of . . . because of it's Connie who's always bringin' up this stuff about vampires and everything . . . telling everybody about vampires and make them think and everything. My text-to-self connection is like how before Halloween everybody thinks about scary things. I do too before Halloween, like about scary things, um costumes and [Tyrone says "uh-huh"] everything. Tyrone.

Tyrone: Um, so I agree with Newman. I thought everybody loves to think about scary things. But, who's that Mr. Dink guy, Doug's next-door neighbor? I think he's like sorta weird because he's like . . . he's like . . . thinks like a kid. He's at all the parties. He like . . . has a machine and that machine makes Doug think Skeeter's more a . . . the, um, vampire. 'Cause like he puts a pumpkin in and the pumpkin comes out with Skeeter's face as a vampire. So I think that Skeeter was a yam . . . I thought that Skeeter was a vampire, but then . . . um . . . as I read into the book I started thinking that it wasn't, because it started pulling away from Skeeter and started going to Patty. So I think . . . at first I thought that it really was Connie, because at first Connie came up with the idea and no one ever checked Connie. Newman's gonna take it away.

The book talk continues . . .

3

The Early Literacy Club
Building Excellence
Through Collaboration

Jane Ching Fung

Teacher networks are the focus of Jane Fung's action research study. For almost ten years, Fung has led the Early Literacy Club, a support network for new teachers. Her study takes us through a year in the life of the network and shows the importance and complexity of new-teacher induction. Her story makes clear how poorly the workplace is structured to handle new-teacher induction. It also shows that learning to teach takes time and lots of support, and that when teachers take induction on as their professional responsibility, everyone benefits.

Fung's data are drawn primarily from the network members' journal writings as well as from interviews, observations, and documents created by the network. We chose this study because it is such a well-told story of a network's growth and of the power of community. Her thoughtful notes take the reader on her journey and help us to understand the importance of leadership. 🍎

Purpose/Rationale

Every year, California hires thousands of brand-new teachers to fill its teaching positions. Many of those newly hired teachers enter the classroom with little or no training in the field of education. My concern, as a mentor teacher and former emergency credential teacher, is that these new educators receive adequate support and are provided with professional development opportunities to help them become effective members of our profession.

41

In 1997, our school district published and distributed District Student Learning Standards to each teacher, parent, and staff member, with little opportunity for training or articulation. The year in which I conducted this study, the district's focus was on the new state English Language Arts Content Standards, with an emphasis on teaching reading. Teachers are expected to create, teach, and assess standards-based lessons. This is not an easy task for an experienced and trained educator, so you can imagine how difficult it would be for a new teacher. Many non-credentialed teachers do not have a chance to take a reading methods class until their second or third year of teaching. We need to find a way to train new teachers now, so that our students receive quality instruction.

I teach in an urban primary school located near downtown Los Angeles. Approximately 85 percent of our school population consists of limited-English-speaking students. Almost all of our students receive free or reduced-price meal tickets. Over 60 percent of the teachers at my school are on emergency credentials and have taught less than three years. Although these new teachers are eager to learn and develop their craft, there are few opportunities in our district and at the school site to meet and collaborate on an ongoing basis.

In 1994, a group of new teachers and I created the Early Literacy Club (ELC), a teacher network at our school. Initially, the goal of the ELC was to provide much-needed instructional and emotional support for the overwhelmed new teacher. With student achievement in state standards a central focus of our state and district, I wanted to research the impact that ongoing collaboration in a teacher network has on new teachers' understandings and use of state standards in classroom practice.

Research Questions

To implement my research, I formulated the following questions:

- Does participation in a collegial network affect new teachers' use of state standards in classroom practice?

42

- How familiar are new teachers with the state standards in language arts?
- Do new teachers use state standards in instructional planning?
- Do new teachers know how to incorporate state standards into classroom instruction?
- How does network participation contribute to the professional development of a new teacher?
- Are new teachers implementing standards-based instruction in their classrooms as a result of network participation?
- What are some ways to manage and lead a teacher network effectively?

Review of Literature

Supply and Demand in the California Teaching Profession

By 2005, California will need to hire approximately 190,000 new teachers to fill its classrooms (Shields, Marsh, and Powell 1998). "Three key factors are fueling the increased demand for teachers: student enrollment growth, class size reduction, and attrition/retirement" (9). Although the California Commission on Teacher Credentialing annually issues enough new teaching credentials to fill classroom vacancies, not all newly credentialed teachers accept teaching positions. Several factors contribute to their decision not to enter the profession: choosing to limit the job search to schools close to home, preferring to work in a suburban setting, and/or being unable to find their preferred teaching assignment (subject or grade level).

In urban and rural areas, the need for teachers is particularly great because of a growing student population and the class-size reduction mandate, forcing communities to hire a large number of noncredentialed teachers. The majority of California's emergency teachers work in urban districts, with 40 percent of all emergency credentialed teachers in California working in the Los Angeles Unified School District.

43

Teacher Preparation

With the large increase in noncredentialed teachers in Los Angeles, the traditional full-time teacher preparation program has given way to a part-time night program. Yet in spite of increased teacher demand in California, the California State University and the University of California have not increased their capacity to prepare more teachers (Shields, Marsh, and Powell 1998); therefore, many emergency teachers are enrolled in private institutions or alternative internship programs. Emergency teachers learn as they go, taking methods courses while actually teaching in the classroom. They are teaching in classrooms with little or no supervision or support; nevertheless, they are expected to perform like their experienced colleagues and to prepare students to master state standards and curriculum.

New-Teacher Induction

New teachers are more likely to be assigned to urban inner-city schools where students tend to be from low-income, disadvantaged minority homes. Of new teachers who enter the profession, about 30 percent leave the profession in the first few years if they are not given support in those crucial years (Darling-Hammond 1997b). Numbers may be even higher in some parts of California, with "CSU's Institute for Education Reform reporting that fifty percent of all new teachers leave the profession within the first five years" (Shields, Marsh, and Powell 1998, 11). Research also shows that careful attention and support given to teachers during their first years of teaching can reduce attrition rates and enhance teachers' performance. New teachers who have "continuous support from a skilled mentor are less likely to leave the profession (attrition rates often drop to about 5 percent, even in cities), and supported novices are much more likely to get beyond classroom management concerns to focus on student learning" (Darling-Hammond 1998, 9).

Quality Professional Development

Professional development opportunities for teachers typically consist of a few days each year at the beginning and/or end of the school year with little or no follow-up (Shields, Marsh, and Powell 1998). Other common professional development practices are daylong or one-shot workshops that have very little effect on classroom practice (Darling-Hammond 1998). "Teachers need to develop their expertise in supportive, long-term professional relationships that focus on developing an understanding of how instruction impacts learning in specific ways" (Cunningham and Allington 1999, 269). New vehicles for effective professional development include teacher networks, teacher academies, professional development schools, national board certification, teaching teams, action research projects, and school study groups (Darling-Hammond 1998). These professional growth opportunities allow teachers to connect learning to classroom practice, link subject matter to instructional strategies, be informed by current research, and engage in ongoing conversations and peer feedback.

Teachers need to discuss their teaching and have ongoing professional discussions with peers, not just read or hear about best practices. New teachers must be given opportunities to "see" what quality teaching looks like in action and be given feedback on their own teaching. "Teachers, like students, learn by working together and reflecting with one another" (Snyder 1999, 7). Teachers and schools involved in these forms of professional development have frequently shown increased student achievement.

Tools

The Early Literacy Club has nine participating members, two mentor teachers and seven members with teaching experience ranging from three months to three years. All members contributed to the data I have collected. In completing my action research project, I used the following four sources of information:

questionnaires, classroom observations, documents created by the network, and teacher reflections.

Questionnaires

Each of the members completed two questionnaires, one in the fall of 1998 and the other in May of 1999. The fall questionnaire surveyed new teachers on their knowledge of state standards in language arts, and determined whether they were currently implementing standards-based instruction in their classroom. The second questionnaire was more in-depth and asked new teachers to assess changes in their understanding of standards-based instruction as a result of network participation. Participants were also asked how the network contributed to their professional growth and classroom practice as well as their goals in the profession.

Classroom Observations

New teachers in the network were invited to observe in other members' classrooms on an ongoing basis. All agreed to an open-door policy, where members were welcome to do informal observations and provide feedback. Our school is on a year-round schedule, so off-track (not teaching) teachers were provided with many opportunities to visit their colleagues who were in the classroom. Teachers also made visitations to other schools in the district during off-track time to observe other mentor teachers as well.

Documents Created by the Network

Members in the network agreed to produce two documents: a Language Arts Standards Time Line and a Language Arts Standards Resource Guide for Teachers. The time line provides a sequential listing of standards to guide instruction over an eight-month period. The resource guide was done cooperatively; each member was assigned a specific language arts standard to research and to develop instructional strategies and activities. The resource guide included an assessment component to measure students' mastery of state standards. Teachers tested, revised, and edited the classroom strategies listed for each standard.

Teacher Reflections

Members were asked to reflect on each monthly meeting informally through group discussions and formally through email and journal writing. They were invited to share any concerns, questions, or comments about the networking process. This was not mandatory. All members have an Early Literacy Club binder for organizing information, and many have their own reflective journals for noting thoughts and information.

Data

Meetings

Ten formal meetings were held throughout the school year on Saturdays and Sundays. Saturday meetings were held at the school site with the permission of the administrator. Sunday meetings were held at network members' homes. Occasionally, the network would meet at the Central Public Library. The three- to four-hour meetings were structured in the following format:

- First Hour: Free Forum
  Network participants shared challenges and ideas about instructional practice, while peers offered feedback and suggestions.
- Following Hours: Language Arts Standards Focus
  Network members chose a Language Arts strand to research and share back with the group. Members introduced one standard from their strand during each meeting. Colleagues provided additional insight and shared instructional strategies for teaching the standard.
- Wrap-Up: Evaluation and Next Steps

To give the reader a sense of how these meetings developed, I describe five of the weekend meetings. They give a sense of the evolution of the group.

First Meeting: Standards, Action Plan, and Teacher Survey
Teachers met to discuss the California English Language Art
Standards and Language Arts Framework. Two years ago, four
network members created a time line for teaching the English
Language Art Standards. The pacing plan had been shared with
other teachers in the district and was used by many teachers at
the school. Although the document was found to be useful, some
thought it was not comprehensive enough. I suggested to the
members that we revisit the Language Arts Standards pacing
plan and add other important concepts and skills that we felt
needed to be included. I also shared that I would be conducting action research and needed some initial data from the teachers. Teachers completed a teacher survey. We agreed to meet at
the Central Library on a Sunday and discuss the standards and
create a time line for introducing them.

New teachers: New teachers filled out the survey and remained
quiet during the discussion. One new teacher had just started
teaching midyear and was overwhelmed with classroom planning, but eager to learn.

Second-year teachers: One second-year teacher had been involved in the network the previous year; the other was new to
the school. Both were fairly quiet during the meeting. They
agreed to working on the standards and filled out the teacher
survey.

Third-year teachers: The three third-year teachers had participated in the network last year. They were more involved in the
conversation and freely expressed themselves throughout the
meeting. One teacher was involved in creating the first Language Arts Standards time line and agreed that it would be beneficial to revisit it and discuss the standards more deeply.

My reflections: I felt that the group was looking toward me for
direction. I was the senior teacher and had been leading the
network for the past four years. I wanted the group to move toward a more collaborative state. The English Language Art Standards were a focus in our district and school. I thought it would
be beneficial to involve all the members in looking at standards

more closely and to develop strategies that we would be able to use in our classrooms. I knew I wanted to conduct action research on this topic, so I asked for an initial self-assessment from teachers about their knowledge of standards. I was happy that the group agreed to participate. I did not want to assign a topic for the network, but I was the mentor and felt that I should suggest topics for discussions. The standards were still pretty new to all of us, and I thought this would benefit the entire group.

Second Meeting: English Language Arts Standards K–2, Stanford Nine Testing Planning Guide, and Grade-Level Pacing Action Plan

We met at the Central Library and read over copies of the state standards. The group then divided into three grade-level groups, from kindergarten through second grade. Each group took the standards and divided them among eight months of instruction. Groups were assigned to develop a pacing plan that would introduce more simple standards at the beginning of the year and scaffold more challenging ones throughout the year.

After completing grade-level standards pacing time lines, each group linked the standards to the Stanford Nine standardized test by writing "S9" by the specific standard. Stanford Nine is administered annually to every student in grades 1 and up.

At the conclusion of the meeting, it was decided that at the next weekly after-school meeting, each teacher would select a strand in the standards and do further research about what strategies we could use to teach the standard to our students.

A former teacher at the school also joined us for this meeting. She was an original network member but had transferred to a school closer to home and did not meet with the group regularly.

New teachers: The new teachers formed the kindergarten group. One teacher had been teaching kindergarten since the beginning of the year, while the other new teacher had arrived midyear. They were team teaching in the same room and were friends prior to teaching at the school. The former teacher from the school who had joined us for the day led the kindergarten group. She had gone through the process of developing a pacing plan before and helped lead the group. The two new teachers expressed their gratitude and relief that someone with more experience was in their group. They stated that they followed her lead and listened to her share her thoughts. Both felt as if they were not much help in the process, but learned a lot from discussing what the standards are and when they should be introduced.

The new teacher who had entered midyear was a bit over-whelmed. She was eager to learn but felt she did not have much to contribute to the process. Her team partner also felt a little lost on the standards, but wanted to become better informed about what they were.

Second-year teachers: The second-year teachers joined in the discussions, but let the third-year teachers lead the conversations. Both second-year teachers remained rather quiet. The one new to our school attended the meetings but did not engage in much conversation with the other teachers. The other second-year teacher was shy by nature. She took a lot of notes but did not say much. They both participated in the grade-level groups, but let the third-year teachers dominate.

Third-year teachers: The third-year teachers were the leaders of the groups. They were more confident and had more class-room experience and knowledge of the state standards. One teacher had been through the process before and felt comfortable making suggestions to the group.

My reflections: I felt that we had a good start. Each group took charge of their task and completed it. I could easily have developed the standards pacing plan myself. I knew that this was challenging, but I wanted them to partake in the process. Now that we had created a time line for teaching the standards, I wanted to lead the teachers in looking deeper into what the standards were. I had never "assigned" homework to the new teachers before. Up until now, I did most of the research and sharing of information and practices. It will be interesting to see what the teachers come up with.

Third Meeting: English Language Art Standards,
Strands, and Strategies

Prior to the third meeting, at a weekly after-school meeting, each teacher chose a strand from the English Language Art Standards to do further research on. The strands were divided into Reading 1.0 (Word Analysis); Reading 2.0 (Comprehension); Reading 3.0 (Literary Response); Writing 1.0 (Writing Mechanics); Writing 2.0 (Writing Domains); and Listening and Speaking. All teachers selected a strand that they were interested in and shared the information at the third meeting.

New teachers' response: When one of the new teachers shared her information, she was apologetic at first. She had only been teaching for a few months and used the books she had from her teacher education classes to gather information about the standard. The other members assured her that we did not expect her to know everything and that we were here to learn together. Other teachers chimed in with their knowledge of the standard and suggested some strategies she could add that would help students master the standard. She felt relieved that she did not have the burden of coming up with instructional strategies all by herself and noted the comments from other teachers so that she could use them in her classroom.

Second-year teachers' response: One second-year teacher introduced her standard and shared what she thought the standard meant to her. Then she listed activities she used in her classroom that were linked to that standard. The other second-year teacher also shared her standard the same way. She was a little less enthusiastic about her work and had only jotted down a few suggestions about the standard.

Third-year teachers' response: The third-year teachers shared their work in a similar manner. One of them related her strategies to research she had read in one of her master's classes. Another shared the method she used with her students.

My response: I felt a bit uneasy about this meeting. There had been some "conflict" brewing among network members about who was producing and who was not. The network initially started off as a support group for new teachers. New teachers were not accountable for any tasks and were free to take or share information that they felt would improve their instruction. The meetings were not structured around a topic and were kept informal so that teachers had the freedom to discuss any topic they wanted. With the focus now on standards and developing a document that we would all use, members were being held responsible for doing their share.

Trust was also becoming an issue that needed to be discussed. When the network began five years earlier, it was with a small group of new teachers who had established a working and social relationship over the years. We were friends off and on campus. The past year brought some changes to the network; three teachers had moved away and new teachers had joined the group. I had not provided time for the group to get to know each other and establish a community. I thought this might have been the reason that conflicts between members started to surface.

As a result of this meeting, members shared individually that they felt other members were not pulling their weight on this project. They claimed it was unfair that some members always shared teaching strategies while others stayed quiet. Members were beginning to set norms for the group. All the members were not meeting expectations, and this caused a lot of friction. I knew that a specific teacher was the focus of this discussion. She was new to the group and had not yet established relationships with other teachers. As the leader, I was not quite sure what I wanted to do. Do I talk to this teacher privately? Had I pushed members too hard? What was the purpose for the network? Had the network become too large? I didn't want the network to be destroyed, and, as the leader, I needed to rethink what I was doing and where we needed to go.

This conflict continued throughout the next few weeks, and it wasn't getting any better. I knew that for us to work as a team and move forward, something had to change. One option was

to take the teacher who was causing the conflict out of the equation; the other was to revisit the main purpose of the network.
Fourth Meeting: Vision for the Network and What Next?
We started the meeting not by talking about English Language Art Standards but by reevaluating the purpose for the network. I didn't want to, but I had to make a statement and take a stand. I had started the network with a group of teachers for the sole purpose of support and collaboration. I wanted the network to move forward and focus on a specific curricular topic, but I did not really ask members what they wanted. I needed to hear from them now.

All the members agreed that they thought the topic was appropriate and something they all needed to improve their instruction. They wanted to continue to work on English Language Art Standards and strategies.

The next topic I brought up was the vision of the network. I apologized to the group and expressed that the network had taken a wrong turn in that it was not supporting all teachers. Although I wanted members to take control of their own learning, I may not have done this in the most equitable way. Holding all members accountable to the group for the same task may have been a mistake. I had not considered the experience level and needs of each teacher. I restated that the network was established for the purpose of *supporting teachers*, not to add more stress to their lives. Furthermore, we all had different personalities and should not all be expected to "perform" at the same level. It was okay to just come and listen. I had lost sight of this and wanted to clear up any misconceptions that may have occurred. I needed to hear from them, and we needed to focus on where we wanted this network to go from here.

New teachers' response: One first-year teacher felt that she had not contributed enough and felt bad about that. She had just begun teaching and was overwhelmed with classroom issues. She wanted to contribute more, but was unable to do so because of her lack of experience. Focusing on the standards had helped her understand what it was she was expected to do, and she had gained a lot of knowledge from the network.

Second-year teachers' response: A second-year teacher also expressed that she had not participated as much as she would have liked. She was grateful that we had a network where she could come and learn from others. The network had helped her grow tremendously as an educator, but she was shy and not always comfortable in sharing. She was not confident in the worth of what she knew, and therefore usually stayed quiet.

Third-year teachers' response: Third-year teachers agreed that maybe the network should focus more on looking at curriculum and standards rather than the amount of work each member produces.

My response: This meeting brought us back to the process. At the conclusion, members decided that it was important for us to complete the standards time line first and foremost. The time line would help teachers develop a pacing plan for teaching the standards next year. The list of strategies would also benefit their students and practice, but would be better left as an ongoing process where teachers could add to it throughout the year. The focus of the network was to help teachers become more effective instructors, not to measure the amount of work produced. We could still deepen our knowledge of standards and instruction without producing a finished product. I realized that I had begun to focus too much on the product and ignored the process.

Last Meeting: Evaluation and Reflections

During the last meeting, the standards time line was distributed and discussed. Teachers were asked to complete a survey and reflect on the process. We discussed what our next steps would be. The teachers all agreed that they would like to look at student work and teaching strategies more deeply next year. Now that they understood the standards, they wanted to take it a step further and look into how to most effectively teach standards so that students are able to master them.

My response: I think the teachers were very proud of the work they had completed on developing the time line for teaching standards. The process had helped them become more familiar with the state standards, and they had learned how they could incorporate standards in their planning and instruction. I hoped that teachers would be honest when completing the surveys. I was eager to read what they thought about the whole process.

Teacher Reflections

Following are notes from the teachers' journals and reflections during meetings.

First-Year Teachers

First-year teachers generally talked about the support that the network provided. They stated that the network helped them acquire strategies that they were able to use in the classroom, a better understanding of the standards, and knowledge about ways to implement standards-based instruction. Both first-year teachers also expressed gratitude that they now had additional resources (other teachers, professional books, state publications, etc.) to turn to when they had questions and needed help. They also felt that networking and collaborating enabled them to stay in such a lonely and demanding job.

Second-Year Teachers

The second-year teachers also found that networking helped them better understand the Language Arts Standards and incorporate them into classroom instruction. They found that networking with other teachers helped them look more deeply and critically at their students' writing and reading, as well as at their own practice. The teachers also reported that working on the standards alignment project with colleagues required them to do homework and be accountable to peers. As a result of the project, they were more motivated and put more effort into both their teaching and learning. Unlike the first-year teachers, who claimed that emotional support was the major advantage of network participation, second-year teachers learned the more practical skills of how to incorporate standards into lessons.

Third-Year Teachers

The three third-year teachers indicated that professional and personal support and growth in teaching were the main objectives of their participation in the network. They felt the network had challenged them to continue to learn and grow in the profession. One third-year teacher wrote, "Being a part of the Early Literacy Club made me realize that as a new teacher, I was not alone. It got me through my first two years of teaching and now in my third year, I realize that I have grown so much as an educator and that growth is due to my participation in the Early Literacy Club. I learned more from collaborating with my peers than [from] two years of my intern teacher credential program." All three teachers felt that collaborating with colleagues was a positive and stimulating experience that helped them develop as educators. Because they had become more effective classroom teachers, third-year teachers also felt that their students benefited greatly from their involvement in the network. "Most of what I incorporate in my classroom is stuff that the Early Literacy Club has contributed. I love the Early Literacy Club!"

Mentor Teachers

As one of the two mentor teachers involved in the network, I found that network participation not only helped me develop my own leadership and facilitation skills, but I, too, gained knowledge and support from those meetings. Working collaboratively with other teachers not only helped me better understand the new state standards, but gave me the opportunity to open my classroom and welcome new educators into a professional culture of collaboration rather than isolation. I was able to demonstrate lessons for teachers, debrief with them afterward, and help them plan lessons for their own students. After trust had been established, the new teachers allowed me to observe them teach. Observing others teach was just as much a learning experience for me as it was for them. I was able to share my observations with the teachers in order to improve their practice, and I gained ideas for my class-room use as well.

The other mentor teacher said that she had taken a long break from professional development and was eager to collaborate and learn from others. She had recently become a mentor and wanted to become more familiar with the new standards in order to help her mentees understand them. As a kindergarten teacher with a unique work schedule, she often felt isolated from the other teachers during the school day. The network meetings allowed her to share her years of experience as well as her questions and concerns. She was unable to attend the weekend meetings because of family obligations, but she was able to meet with the network during the week at the school site.

Teacher Questionnaire Results

In July, at the beginning of the school year, and in May, at the end, Early Literacy Club members were asked to respond to the following questions about their network participation and professional growth:

1. How familiar are you with the state English Language Arts Standards?
2. Do you use standards in your instructional planning currently?
3. Do you know how to incorporate standards into your instruction?
4. How would you rate yourself as an effective literacy teacher?

First-Year Teachers
In July, first-year teachers reported that they had seen the English Language Art Standards but were not familiar with them and did not currently use them in their instructional planning. They stated that they did not know how to incorporate them in their instruction. They felt they were ineffective literacy teachers.

By May, these first-year teachers were asked to respond to the same questions. Both reported that they now knew what the

English Language Arts Standards were and were using them regularly in their planning and instruction. One first-year teacher reported that she had developed to a great degree as a literacy instructor, while the other teacher felt that she had shown improvement.

Second-Year Teachers

In July, a second-year teacher reported that she was not familiar with the standards and did not use them in her lesson planning. She said that she had little understanding about how to incorporate them in her instruction. She felt that she was not an effective literacy teacher. In May, the same teacher reported that she had a better understanding of the state standards and how to incorporate them into her practice. She also felt that she had shown development in her effectiveness as a literacy instructor.

The other second-year teacher reported in July that she was familiar with the standards and used them in her planning, but was not sure about how to incorporate them into her instruction. She also felt that she was somewhat effective as a literacy teacher. In her May response, the same teacher reported that she had developed to a great degree as a literacy teacher and was regularly using standards in her instructional planning. She also reported that she was learning how to incorporate the standards into her practice.

Third-Year Teachers

In July, the third-year teachers reported that they had read the standards and used them somewhat in their instructional planning. They were unsure about how to incorporate the standards into their classroom practice and were not very confident about the relationship between the implementation of standards and student outcomes. Two of the three teachers reported that they were somewhat effective as literacy teachers, while one teacher rated herself as ineffective.

In response to the May questionnaire, the third-year teachers indicated they were more familiar with the state standards and were using them in their instructional planning. Two of the three teachers were aware of how to incorporate the standards into classroom practice, while the other teacher reported that she was learning how to incorporate the standards into her practice. All three teachers claimed they had developed as more skillful literacy instructors.

Mentor Teachers

In July, both mentor teachers wrote that they had read and understood the state standards. One teacher was using standards in instructional planning and knew how to incorporate them into practice. She rated herself as an effective literacy instructor with extensive training in reading instruction. The same teacher reported in May that participating in the network helped her refine her practice and increase her understanding of the state standards.

The other mentor teacher wrote that she had partially incorporated the state standards in her planning and instruction. She felt she was an effective literacy teacher. After her involvement in the network, she reported in May that she had gained a better understanding about how to incorporate standards-based instruction in her classroom and that she had improved as a literacy instructor.

All network members credited the Early Literacy Club with contributing to their professional development and implementation of state standards in classroom practice. They expressed a desire to continue participating in the network the next school year. The teachers reported that their involvement in the network led them to seek other opportunities for networking and collaboration. Most reported that they had joined other district and university networks in addition to the Early Literacy Club.

Analysis

My data suggest that by participating in the Early Literacy Club network, the teachers have:

- shown improvement in their professional practices
- gained a deeper understanding of state standards and subject matter

- had an opportunity to collaborate with peers regularly
- gained confidence in their own teaching
- acquired and participated in creating teaching resources
- found a readily available support system
- sought further professional development in addition to the network
- taken on leadership roles both at school and in the profession
- reported greater job satisfaction.

Professional Development

These data also suggest some important lessons about professional development for new and experienced teachers. The first lesson is the power of networking. These teachers came on their own time during weekends over the course of a year. There were extrinsic rewards attached to their participation. They worked through some difficult personal relationships related to high expectations for the group and what they hoped to learn from it. They achieved their goals, and, along the way, they discovered the importance of process in community. Each of them emerged from the experience with a better sense of the literacy curriculum, with increased competence as teachers, and with a desire to continue to work with other teachers in this way.

I also learned about leadership development, especially the importance of keeping your purpose clear. Despite our name, we were not coming together primarily to develop literacy curricula. We were first and foremost a support group for new teachers. When we let the product drive our work, our ability to relate with one another and to support each other was compromised. When I was able to expose this problem to the group, the tension was resolved and we were more productive.

Job Satisfaction and Professional Growth

The network experience impacted teachers' commitment to staying in education. The members of the network are more actively involved in the profession than their new-teacher counterparts who decided not to partake in the network. All members have engaged in professional development outside of the network such as joining other subject-matter associations, university projects, and professional affiliations. Many have presented workshops and inservice sessions at both the district and state level. All of the network participants expressed their desire to continue working with the ELC during the next school year. Some expressed a wish to contribute more to the network in the coming year and found it satisfying when they were asked to take on more responsibilities.

Such commitment to the profession is not the usual outcome of staff development projects. I think that finding a way to bring each voice into the discussion and to draw on the experience, however limited, of each participant, enriched all and enhanced our self-confidence. Although the network was made available to all new teachers at the school, two of them chose not to participate. Both of these teachers have left permanent positions in the classroom, and have opted to become substitute teachers instead. Teacher networks are a valuable tool in retaining and supporting new teachers. Based on our experience, the voluntary nature of the network is integral to its success.

New Questions for Research

New-teacher participation in a network has certainly made a positive impact in the lives of the teachers involved. The next step is to see what results new-teacher participation in a network has on student achievement. We need to focus on how to best assimilate teachers' knowledge of standards into student achievement. Some possible questions to consider are: Do students of teachers involved in a literacy network show improvement in literacy? Do students show greater interest in language arts as a result of teacher participation in the network? Do students notice a difference in teaching style after participation in the network?

Policy Implications

The more knowledgeable and successful we are as educators, the more our students will achieve. My study shows the importance of ongoing support and collaboration in the training and retention of new teachers. Networks are one way to improve our teaching practices and train new teachers in a comfortable, risk-free environment. I would like to offer the following suggestions for policy implications:

- Provide opportunities during the school day for teachers to collaborate on an ongoing basis.
- Support teachers who choose to collaborate.
- Fund more teacher networks.
- Include networks as an option for new-teacher support in the mentor program.
- Provide opportunities for preservice teachers to become actively involved in teacher networks.

Update

As of spring 2002, all nine Early Literacy Club members remain classroom teachers. The network is now a cross-school network and has increased its membership to fourteen. Membership includes: National Board Certified teachers, mentor teachers, literacy and math facilitators, and teacher leaders. The network continues to meet regularly with members' teaching experience ranging from three weeks to fourteen years. The current focus of the network is individual teacher action research. The network's motto remains: *The Early Literacy Club: Building Excellence through Collaboration.*

4

The Mother Tongue

The Role of Parent-Teacher Communication in Helping Students Reach New Standards

Lara Goldstone

Lara Goldstone conducted her action research on how to help children achieve standards. Meeting the performance standard related to speaking and listening was a great challenge for her primarily Asian American students because it was in direct conflict with the cultural norms of their community. Her research points to the importance of home-school partnerships and challenges the existing conditions of the workplace. She calls for additional resources to help non-English-speaking parents support their children's achieving standards. This support could include translations of standards for the various language groups in the school, extending the time and availability of parent-teacher conferences, and providing translators during conferences.

Drawing on in-class discussions, notes from parent conferences, and surveys of students and parents, Goldstone found that when parents are made aware of the standards and taught how to reinforce them at home, students achieve them. 🍎

Research Question

What happens when I communicate explicitly with parents about the New Middle School English Language Arts Standards for Student Achievement? More specifically, what is the impact of parental understanding of the new standards for speaking and listening on their children's performance?

Rationale

I teach a humanities block to two classes of sixth graders at a small middle school in Manhattan's Chinatown, and these sixty-six students, their work, and their parents are the subject of my study. Approximately 80 percent of the students are Chinese or Chinese American. The other 20 percent are Puerto Rican, Ecuadorian, African American, and Caucasian. Approximately half are girls.

When confronted for the first time with the ambitious work that Community School District 2 had done with the New Standards, I was inspired to try a new approach to teaching that emphasized discussing clear benchmarks of performance with the students, who would then revise their work until it was "good enough." Though such criteria-based work was tremendously helpful in improving my students' reading and writing, I was disappointed that most of my students did not meet the performance standards for speaking and listening.

To meet the speaking and listening standards, students must participate actively in discussions. In the increasingly diverse cultural landscape of the United States, verbal communication is more challenging and necessary than ever before. Middle school–age students of today will be required to express their ideas verbally not only to gain admission to competitive high schools and colleges, but also to maintain jobs in an economy that has come to value "soft" skills such as teamwork and communication (Murane and Levy 1997). Hence, it is appropriate that the New Standards for Middle School adopted by New York City include a performance standard for speaking and listening that requires students to participate in group meetings and meet several criteria: to take turns, solicit other students' opinions and comments, offer their own opinions without dominating, respond appropriately to comments and questions, give reasons and evidence to support opinions, and clarify and expand when asked to do so (New York City Board of Education 1997, 24).

Last year, I held class discussions three to four times a week, had students model each of the above criteria, and facilitated student reflections on their progress in discussions. By the end of June, most students recognized that they had not even come close to "good enough" speaking and were unable to meet the standards.

Why, I wondered all summer, had I not been able to train effective speakers? I suspected that there might have been a clash between our district's expectations and those of the students' parents. Many of the students have been educated at home and in more traditional Chinatown schools to believe that it is more appropriate to work quietly and not speak up, not to openly disagree with others, and not to speak without being called on. Might this cultural mismatch have been a factor? And, if so, could communication about the speaking standards with my students' parents, who have been very supportive of my work with their children, help achievement? With this query in mind, I set out to find out more about parental involvement and to design a course of action.

Review of the Literature

The Institute for Learning at the University of Pittsburgh has published several documents based on teaching "accountable talk" in New Standards test sites, including some schools in my district. First, their research shows the benefits of speaking on reasoning ability and literacy (Institute for Learning 1998a). In addition, this research demonstrates that explicit criteria and modeling are essential in getting students to reach the New Standards for speaking and listening (Institute for Learning 1998b, 1998c). Despite these convincing pieces of evidence, there is no specific mention of the need for parent involvement in helping children to reach the New Standards or on how to support second-language learners.

The tremendous body of research on second-language learners and speaking makes it clear that students whose first language is not English often have difficulty speaking in English about academic topics such as those prescribed in the New Standards (Cummins 1981; Krashen 1981b), even if they seem to have no trouble socializing and communicating about nonacademic topics. According to James Cummins, it takes immigrant students considerably longer (five to seven years) to develop age-appropriate academic skills in English than to develop age-appropriate communicative skills in English (approximately two years). Furthermore, the "affective filter"—the fear or embarrassment that keeps language learners from speaking when worried about mistakes—increases considerably at puberty (Elkind 1970; Krashen 1981a, 1981c).

Epstein (1987) reports that homework is often the only form of serious communication about school and learning between parents and school-aged children, even when children need help. As such, assigning homework alone is not a very effective way of helping parents to help their children. Epstein also found that teachers most often ask parents to help only students who are considered discipline problems. "The parents of other children say they could spend more time helping their children at home if they were shown how to do so. There is a supply of 'untapped' parental assistance available to teachers which may be especially useful in improving the skills of 'average' students who could do better with additional time and attention" (128).

Research shows that even when parents do help their children with homework, they have rarely been shown how to help their children develop needed skills. Parental discussions of school with children do correlate with increased achievement. Children who like to talk about school with their parents and who are not tense working with their parents on home learning activities have higher reading and math skills (Epstein 1988). In addition, when parents are informed about the best ways to encourage their children in school, they are in a better position to assist them (Kellaghan, et al. 1993).

Lily Wong Fillmore (1990) reports that children earning higher grades and test scores tend to be from homes where the values and ways of learning match those at school. If the family's approach to life and learning is very different from that encouraged in school, children are less likely to do well. For example, children whose parents encourage them to be quiet and not disagree with others may be reluctant to engage in discussions and debates in class. Children whose families reinforce good work and study habits at home, emphasize the value of education, and express high expectations tend to do well (Henderson and Berla 1994). James Comer's study (1988) shows that children learn from people with whom they bond. That is, children will be able to reconcile their experiences at home and at school more easily if their parents and schools collaborate to bridge the gap between the mainstream American school and the home culture.

Working-class Asian students who defy trends of poor achievement usually associated with low SES are often cited in such studies. However, I found no research on the achievement of Asian American students with respect to speaking in class.

The Study

Data Collection Categories

My data collection falls into three categories: assessment of student achievement during discussions, notes from communication with parents about the speaking standards, and written and spoken comments from parents and students about speaking.

Assessment of Student Achievement

This year, we added a grade for discussions on the students' report cards. For each student, I recorded a grade (4 = meets all criteria, 3 = meets most of the criteria, 2 = meets some of the criteria, and 1 = meets barely any of the criteria) for discussions and wrote explicit comments about the student's performance. I was able to aggregate this data from quarters one through three to find trends in student achievement. To help me understand more specifically which criteria for speaking the students were and were not meeting, I regularly assessed students' discussion abilities by using a check-off sheet during discussions that lists the criteria for good discussions as prescribed in the New Standards document. I also audiotaped discussions from the first three quarters and analyzed the tapes using the same criteria.

Communication with Parents

Most of my students' parents speak Cantonese, making it difficult for me to communicate with them. Our school has a bilingual school aide whose schedule permits her to translate a minimal amount of parent letters and to help translate parent-teacher conferences in all six of our school's classrooms. In order to accommodate every parent who wanted a conference and to comply with the teacher's contract, our director scheduled five-minute parent-teacher conferences during one afternoon and one evening in both November and February. For the purposes of my study, I made a point of focusing my comments during these conferences on the children's discussions grade, often going way over the five-minute time limit in order to explain why this skill is important and how parents can help their children improve. I also tended to monopolize the bilingual school aide, who was supposed to travel around equally between classrooms but obliged me by translating for my conferences most of the time. I took notes from these conferences, including the actual length of each conference.

Reflections from Students and Parents

After each quarter, I asked students to write a reflection on their participation in discussions, explaining what they think their discussions grade should be and what has influenced their performance. I also asked parents to fill out a survey about their children's discussions abilities during the second quarter and after the third quarter.

Data

Overall, my students' abilities to meet the criteria for speaking improved over the first three quarters. In the first quarter, only six out of sixty-six students met most of the criteria, and twenty-four met none. By the third quarter, fifty-two students met most of the criteria, and only four met none (see Table 4–1).

Table 4–1 Student Achievement of Speaking Standards Over Time ($n = 66$)

Report Card Grade in Speaking	1st Quarter	2nd Quarter	3rd Quarter
4 (meets all criteria)	0	2	16
3 (meets most of criteria)	6	19	36
2 (meets some of criteria)	36	31	10
1 (meets barely any of criteria)	24	14	4

During the first quarter, twenty-four students (approximately twelve in each class) never participated significantly in discussions. Most of the comments of those who did speak during discussions consisted of students making points unrelated to previous remarks and unsupported by evidence or elaboration (see Table 4–2). By the second quarter, ten of the twenty-four nonparticipants began participating in discussions, and more of the remarks met the criteria for good speaking. During the third quarter, approximately 95 percent of all remarks fit the New

Table 4–2 Most Common Types of Remarks During Student Discussions

Type of Remark	% of Remarks of This Type		
	1st Q	2nd Q	3rd Q
Makes a relevant but disconnected statement	78	38	5
Clarifies a statement by another*	5	5	5
States a disagreement with an idea*	3	10	20
Supports statement with evidence or example*	5	20	22
Builds on another students' remark*	2	10	30
Makes a connection between topic and another text, issue, etc.*	5	10	7
Raises a question that furthers the discussions*	0	3	5
Responds effectively to a disagreement with previous comment*	0	3	17

*remark fits the New Standards criteria

Standards speaking criteria, and all but four students participated significantly. Of the four students who would never speak, two of them did not have parent-teacher conferences.

Communication with Parents

The average length of my first-quarter conferences was ten to twelve minutes, more than twice the allotted time of five minutes. Conferences after the second quarter were a bit shorter, since I needed only to reiterate the ideas about discussions I had told most parents already. In order to discuss each student's strengths and areas for improvement individually, I asked the school aide to translate for me for about half of the conferences—specifically, those for students who had received a 1 or 2 in discussions on their report cards—and frequently asked capable seventh-grade students to translate during the other half.

My notes from parent-teacher conferences reveal several patterns among parental views about student discussions.

- Many parents said that they knew speaking was important but indicated that they do not encourage their children to speak at home. Some parents said they have too many children around and when they are tired they would prefer a quiet home.
- Frequently, parents were dismayed by their children's silence during discussions, because they hear their children being very talkative at home and do not understand why their child would not speak in class.
- Repeatedly, after listening to me explain the notion of debating and disagreeing in discussions, parents would tell me that they have taught their children not to disagree openly. Parents said that in the Chinese culture it is considered disrespectful, particularly for children, to argue or speak out against another person.

Reflection of Students and Parents

Student reflections from the first, second, and third quarters indicate a growing awareness of the criteria for good speaking and how the students measure up to the standards. After the first

70

quarter, students frequently commented that they needed to speak "more," but by the third quarter, students wrote about specific ways in which they had improved or still needed to improve. Some students felt that they were about to state their position, back it up with evidence, and expand on others' comments. Other students believed that they improved the type of questions they ask, as well as their ability to draw others into the discussion. Some students, however, said that they still become flustered when other students disagree with them and feel they would like to learn how to defend their position in an argument.

Parental surveys also indicate a growing agreement about the importance of speaking. On the second-quarter surveys, twenty of the sixty-three parents who responded deemed speaking well "very important," but by the third quarter surveys, that number had increased to forty-seven of the sixty-two parents who responded. Six parents still indicated that speaking was "not important" on the third-quarter surveys. In addition, parental surveys support the patterns I noticed from my conference notes about reasons for student silence. Parents attribute their children's quietness in discussions to fear of making mistakes (23 percent of parents), concern about respect (17 percent), difficulty putting ideas into words (25 percent), and shyness (35 percent) (see Figure 4–1).

Case Studies

In order to elucidate the various factors of this standards-based equation, I have chosen three students whose growth in speaking over the course of the three quarters typified that of many students and whose challenges represent the breadth of those my class encountered. All three began with a 1 in speaking. A brief summary of what transpired with each of these three students follows.

Student 1

Student 1 is a very capable reader and writer who exhibits confidence and risk taking with her written work. During the first

Figure 4–1 Reasons Parents Give to Explain Their Children's Difficulties with Discussion

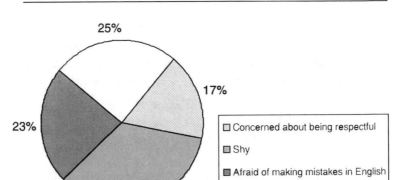

two quarters, she seemed to be focused on the discussions, making eye contact with the speakers and turning to quoted paragraphs in the text, but she never spoke up in discussions. She confided in me at several points during the year about feelings of insecurity and worries about popularity. Student 1 wrote in her first-quarter reflection, "I am terrible in discussions because I never say anything. I have ideas in my head, but I don't want to share them, because some people might think they're stupid."

During the parent-teacher conference, this student's mother seemed shocked about the low discussions score bobbing in a sea of excellent grades in other areas. "She is so talkative at home. I just don't get it." When the student left the room to go talk to a friend in the hallway, I mentioned to her mom that I suspected Student 1 was worried about her peers' impressions of her, and I suggested that her mom talk to her about that. She agreed. By the second quarter, she still had made no contributions to class discussions. She noted in her reflection, "I still am not participating in discussions. I am not so worried that people will think my ideas are dumb—well, all except one person." In our second parent-teacher conference, Student 1's mother told me, through the translator, "I think she is worried that other kids will laugh at her. Some of the girls in her class are kind of mean and tease a lot. I told her not to worry about them. Her grades are more important. But she still isn't participating."

Between February and April, something changed outside of class. She began to exude a sense of self-confidence in front of her peers that I had not seen before. She also began to speak very actively in discussions. Though she looked nervously at the ground as she expressed very sophisticated ideas, she seemed unconcerned about what others would think about her. In her third-quarter reflection, Student 1 wrote, "I improved this quarter in discussions a lot (*sic*). My mom kept telling me not to care about V___, and I guess I started realizing that she's right. I guess, now I feel comfortable disagreeing with people because well, now I even disagree with my best friend." Student 1 scored a 4 in discussions during the third quarter.

Student 2

Student 2 is a quiet, meticulous student who seems scared of his own shadow. His normal volume is barely audible from only three inches away. His mother works in the lunchroom in our school's building and can often be heard screaming at students who get out of line. He scored a 1 during the first quarter in discussions. He wrote in his first-quarter reflection, "I need to improve in speaking. Sometimes I hear someone say something wrong but I don't want to be rude. Also, sometimes I raise my hand and I don't get called on, so I put my hand down. I know I have to improve because I got a '1' and my mom is going to yell at me." During the parent-teacher conference, I spoke to his mother, who speaks English, about his silence and the district's goals for speaking. "He's not used to speaking, because he keeps real quiet at home," his mother said. I encouraged her to engage her son in conversations about school, the news, and so forth, to get him used to speaking audibly. She agreed but did not seem convinced of the importance of this.

The next quarter, Student 2's grades did not improve. At the second parent-teacher conference, his mother said, "Okay. What can I do? I don't like him getting bad grades. I told him to speak up in discussions, but I guess he isn't." I asked her if he has been raised to be very quiet, and she said that his grandfather is sick, and they have to be quiet in the house. I again suggested that she encourage her son to talk more.

By the third quarter, Student 2 began to talk more during discussions. He never disagreed with another student's point of view, but he would add significantly to the talks. Students would frequently ask him to speak more loudly, and he would repeat more audibly. In his third-quarter reflection, he hinted that his mother was a factor in his improvement: "This quarter, I deserve a 3 in discussions, because now I participate. I think I changed, because now we can talk more around the house, so I am getting used to it. My parents told me to talk more and I tried." He made a 2.5 on the third-quarter grade for discussions.

Student 3

Rebecca is an average student who does her work but has difficulty understanding grade-level texts in English. She struck me as loquacious with her friends on the playground but did not say a word during discussions the first or second quarters. Her mother was baffled. "She talks a lot. Her uncles call her 'Chatterbox.'" She wrote in her first-quarter reflection, "I know I don't talk in discussions. Everyone talks so fast, and sometimes I don't understand what they're saying. When I think of something to say, someone else says it already."

After a second quarter of silence from Student 3, I talked to her uncle about practicing speaking with her about difficult subjects, like what she is learning in school, or the news. He said he would definitely try. She first participated in a discussion in March, and after that first time, she began to speak at least once each discussion. Her remarks began as comments unrelated to other students', but eventually she began to respond to and build on others' comments. Her uncle, it seemed, had helped her: "This quarter, I started to improve in discussions. My uncle helped me by asking me to explain my homework to him, so I got used to talking about school."

Analysis

My data suggests that communication with parents about the New Standards for speaking allowed parents to intervene and help their students to overcome their fears. Through analyzing my conference notes and student reflections, three major barriers to student achievement of the speaking criteria became apparent, complemented by three strategies for overcoming these barriers.

First, some students, like Student 3, do not feel confident speaking about academic subjects in English. Their silence in class baffles their parents, who hear their children prattling on at home and on the phone with their friends. Allowing students time to wait until they feel more comfortable speaking English, creating a classroom environment of mutual trust and respect, giving students separate practice in English language skills, and showing parents how to practice speaking with their children even in their primary language about complex subjects might all help students who are not confident in their academic English abilities. In his third-quarter reflection, one student who showed great improvement in discussions wrote that his parents were now making him speak English with relatives from Singapore about computer equipment, which was helping him feel more comfortable using English in class discussions.

Second, some students, like Student 2, have been reared to believe that voicing disagreement with others constitutes disrespectful behavior or have been conditioned to be very quiet. Students are afraid that they will hurt someone's feelings if they disagree or argue an opposing point. Speaking with parents about why discussions are important in school during conferences helped some students to feel more comfortable speaking up and disagreeing. In particular, parents and children began discussing topics like current events where they disagreed on issues or explored different points of view. Parents were able to explain to their children the difference between respectfully disagreeing in

75

a discussion with peers and disrespectfully arguing in other situations. In addition, practicing as a class ways to disagree politely, when students did not get offended or hurt, helped students to feel more at ease disagreeing.

Third, students such as Student 1 feel shy for a variety of reasons when speaking up in front of their peers. The students are afraid that other students will laugh at them or that their faces will turn red, revealing their discomfort to everyone. Feelings of insecurity are prevalent among adolescents whose identities are changing, and for whom peer approval is of paramount importance. Here again, creating a respectful and trusting classroom environment and having parents work with their children on self-esteem are key.

The disappointingly high number of students who met barely any or none of the criteria for speaking by the third quarter suggests that I could have communicated more successfully with parents. However, there were three major obstacles to successful communication that I alluded to previously:

1. Limited access to translators: My school district does not fund a translator for our school, and our "flex" funds were so tied up in paying for our teaching staff that our budget left no room to hire a translator on an as-needed basis.

2. Limited access to translated materials: The time I spent during parent-teacher conferences explaining the New Standards might have been reduced had I been able to send parents a copy of the New Standards written in Chinese. Though my district is at the national forefront of the work with the New Standards, they have repeatedly neglected to meet my director's requests for a translated copy of the standards documents.

3. Cultural barriers: Though I did manage to convince some parents of the importance of speaking in class, it is difficult to go against deeply ingrained ideas about how children should behave. I believe that some parents truly wanted to help their children improve their speaking grades but could

76

not help their children practice speaking at home, because they were not accustomed to having discussions about academic topics with their children.

In general, where the standard was supported at home, students made gains in classroom discussions and were able to meet most of the speaking criteria.

New Questions for Research

My study encompassed my working environment, which is small and homogeneous compared to many other middle schools. Further research into different strategies for communicating with parents in different settings could prove useful before setting new policies. For example, though I lament the brevity of my parent-teacher conferences, other schools with different scheduling have even shorter time limits. Furthermore, my conclusions about students of Chinese immigrant parents, who tend to take an active role in making sure that their children are meeting the school's standards, might not bear out with students whose parents are less involved; different types of communication might be involved. I propose a few possible questions for further action research:

- What is the effect of block scheduling on parent-teacher communication around standards and student achievement?
- What does effective parent-teacher communication with parents with different communication styles and attitudes toward their involvement in their children's education look like?
- What happens to student achievement when parents attend classes in which *they* learn to master the New Standards of effective communication?

Policy Implications

My study suggests that student achievement increases when students feel comfortable speaking in front of their peers and when teachers communicate standards to parents, thereby indicating the need for policy changes at three different levels.

1. At the classroom instruction level, teachers should carefully cultivate a respectful and caring community in their classrooms. Though some teachers see such work as fluffy or tangential to achievement, it is essential in getting middle school students, especially those who are not confident in their English language abilities, to feel at ease expressing themselves in class. Such work is highly contextual, and there is a plethora of researched and published methods and curricula available for community building in the classroom. Observing expert teachers at the beginning of the year as they work to establish the classroom environment might be very useful as well.

2. At the district level, budgets should ensure funding for translators so that parents from all linguistic and cultural backgrounds can understand the standards and learn how to help their children achieve them.

3. District professional development around standards should include discussions of cultural barriers, accountable talk, and effective communication with parents.

4. Citywide performance standards should be translated into other languages so that all parents can read and understand them.

5. The teacher contract should allocate more time for parent-teacher conferences.

The value of excellent communication skills for students is clear, and I commend the board of education for its adoption of high standards. In order to level the playing field, students from all cultural and linguistic backgrounds must be given equal opportunities to achieve the rigorous criteria set forth in the standards documents. Paving the way for more teacher-parent communication with translators, conference time, and appropriate professional development are the first steps to success.

5

Time and Choice
A Winning Combination

Carol Tureski

My education was the liberty I had to read indiscriminately and all the time, with my eyes hanging out.

—Dylan Thomas

In this chapter, Carol Tureski writes about access to resources that she and her English as a Second Language (ESL) students need to meet language arts standards in high school. Her study highlights some of the obstacles that thoughtful teachers face as they try to teach in ways that they know will work well with their students and support their achievement. The big hurdle that she must overcome relates to conditions of the workplace: an anachronistic system for bringing materials into the classroom and an inflexible schedule. Underlying this is the low status of teachers in the system, manifested here by the fact that teachers cannot even order books appropriate for their students.

We selected this study for inclusion in this book because we particularly liked a number of its features. Tureski begins with a compelling story that frames the problem. Her literature review sets the stage for her study of second-language learners' reading. Her use of surveys of students, teachers, and parents and student logs makes the case for her policy recommendations. Tureski recommends that teachers be included in decisions about school resources—in particular, their selection—and about school schedules.

Imagine for a moment that you are a New York City public school teacher given the opportunity to choose and order books for your high school literature class. The staff person who holds the school's only CD-ROM version of the state approved list is out on jury duty, and no one can tell you for certain when he will be back. So, you hunt down the catalogues in the main office and begin your quest. You hit your first purchasing hurdle when you realize the books are listed only by title. You cannot search for books by subject, reading level, author, theme, or publisher. Since you do not know the exact titles, your search is derailed temporarily. You realize that before you can use the catalogue, you have to identify titles that you think will engage students. Okay. Now you're ready!

No such luck. Many of the titles that you have identified for your students do not appear in the catalogue. You turn to a more seasoned colleague for a clarification. She gives you three possible explanations: It is because the publisher refuses to do business with the board of education because it takes too long to receive payment. Or it is because it was on the list for the past five years, but oddly enough, it doesn't appear this year. Or it is because it's too new to have made the list this year. You begin to catch on to the ordering system. You eliminate books published within the past year from your list because the chances that any have been reviewed, approved by the board, and assigned an order number are slim. You make a note to check back next year.

Finally you strike it big when you find a title from your list, *Black Boy*, by Richard Wright, in the board's listing . . . eight times! Which copy should you order? Since you are limited by a yearly spending cap of $30 per student to cover all their classes and the listing only provides titles without descriptions or photos of this and other books, you decide to order the edition that is priced in the middle between $8.53 to $16.31 and hope for the best. You copy the pertinent information onto an order form, get approval from an administrator, and hand deliver it to the person in charge of placing book orders. You are informed that you might receive your books within one to three months, and you're told to keep your fingers crossed. You walk away shaking your head, knowing that you could have gone to your local bookstore, browsed through a variety of books (even recent publications!), chosen an edition, negotiated a fair price, used the school tax-free number, purchased the books, and had them in your students' hands within a week.

This is the situation that confronts countless elementary, middle, and high school teachers in New York City public schools each year. At one time, I was among them, and I struggled to help my students, who, then as now, are primarily speakers of English as a Second Language (ESL), to become fluent readers of English. My own experience as a reader suggested to me that having time to read is a critical factor, and even more important is deciding what to read.

Background Research

As a teacher of second-language learners, I looked into the research on reading instruction for this specific population. I focused particularly on the issue of learning to read in a second language and searched also for anything that might give me some insight into the ways in which time and choice influence reading achievement.

ESL Students and Reading

Research on reading in the field of English as a Second Language tells us that the process a student uses to read is the same whether reading English as a first or second language (Grabe 1991). For example, most readers essentially use their knowledge of word order, grammar, sound/symbol relationships, and meaning to gain understanding from a text. However, for English-language learners, this task can prove to be more difficult. According to Peregoy and Boyle (1997), two likely reasons for this are students' second-language proficiency level and their background knowledge. ESL students may not have the exposure to idiomatic English expressions such as "Once upon a time"

81

and word groupings such as "Let's go to the movies" to help them read with fluidity. In addition, content material may be unfamiliar to students, thus causing comprehension difficulties. Peregoy and Boyle suggest that in order to offset reading difficulties, ESL teachers should provide reading material with content familiar to their students' lives and interests.

Time Reading in School

Atwell (1998) suggests that there is a general lesson that middle and high school English teachers inadvertently convey to students, which is, "Reading is a waste of English class time." While teachers tend to spend class time on activities to make a book more interesting, to check comprehension, or to test knowledge of assigned reading, actual reading time is not part of class work. This is despite the fact that research, such as that by Ivey (2000), indicates that it is time alone with a book that best helps students to develop interest in reading and make sense of what they read.

Quality time for reading is even less likely to occur for students experiencing reading difficulties (Ivey 2000). Many ESL students, especially newcomers, fall into this category and, like most struggling readers, they are given direct instruction, worksheets, and fragmented pieces of stories and books to read instead of having opportunities to become engaged in reading books.

Choice in Book Selection

Rosenblatt's (1978) research on reading showed that for comprehension to be meaningful, the reader must construct meaning by making connections to the text from personal experience and prior knowledge. No one knows better about these two factors than students themselves and the classroom teachers who work with them daily. Reading materials and/or grade-level texts mandated by district or school administrators rarely take into account the particular needs of students and their teachers. Teachers who find these texts inappropriate to their students' interests and reading levels return countless books to book closets.

Allen (1995) made significant progress with reluctant and low-level adolescent readers when she provided students with a wide array of books from which to choose. Students chose books that were meaningful and significant to them. Allen points out that learning to choose is an essential step in literacy and literacy appreciation.

Context

Spurred on by this research on reading, I realized that the bureaucracy had essentially hamstrung my students and me. I was able to admit to myself that I had not been able to help my students become proficient readers. I became convinced that if they were to try to meet the New York City's High School English Language Arts Performance Standards that require students to read twenty-five books of quality and complexity per school year, my students would have to be given time for reading and choice in their reading selections. In frustration, I looked for another teaching setting—somewhere I could pursue my goal of literacy instruction at the high school level.

In the 2000–2001 school year, I began teaching humanities in an alternative school. It was a radical change from the traditional setting in which I had spent my first years of teaching. Here, the faculty is deeply committed to teacher leadership and school-based management. In this new setting, I was able to explore what happens when students are given both time to read and choice in the selection of their reading material. This is the story of that year.

Setting

Our high school is located on a community college campus and shares some of the college's facilities—including the library. The ESL population at the campus is very large and the books in the section of the library created for this population are in high demand and circulation. In contrast, the bookroom at our school has a small lending library, and the majority of books are of low interest to these young adults. Many are old and yellowed. Ancient copies of Johanna Spyri's *Heidi* are typical of the school's collection.

I asked the team of teachers with whom I work to designate money in the budget to purchase books for a class library. They approved the idea and, based on recommendations from students, teachers, librarians, and bookstore clerks, I pored over catalogues and selected approximately fifty books. In addition, my colleagues and I worked out a schedule that allotted students two seventy-minute periods per week devoted to independent reading. With both time and choice in place, I hoped my students would develop into readers, and I was determined to study the process.

Method

My focus was on the impact of providing students with time and choice in reading. I gathered information from the student participants in the reading program and from their parents and teachers. To do this, I chose a number of research tools.

Book Lists, Reading Logs, Surveys, and Questionnaires

Students kept individual book lists throughout the year to help them keep track of their reading (see Figure 5–1). Their lists provided the following information: the number of books read; the genre, reading level, and length of books; and the time spent reading each book. I also kept a reading log to record books students had finished or abandoned (see Figure 5–2). Students completed a reader's survey, in which they were asked to describe changes in their reading habits between June 2000 and June 2001 (Figure 5–3). We focused on such topics as "time spent reading per week" and "time spent between books."

Figure 5–1 Student Book List

Name: Nathalie _____ Booklist

Bk. #	Title	Author	Genre	# of pgs.	rding. level	Date finished	Project	comments
1	Annies baby	Editor: Beatriz Sparks	Diary Real life	335	average	october	Reading Logs	It was a great book and gave an advice to teenagers.
2	Missing pieces	Norma fox Mazer	Real life fiction	180/150	Easy - average	october	Reading Logs	I didn't like it it was bored and the end could be better.
3.	The outsides	S.E Hinton	Real life fiction	180	Average	Nov.	Book chats	Made me cry.
4.	The giver	Louis Lowery	Fantasy. Sci: fiction	180	Challenging	Nov.	comp. chats	It's a great book hard words and show me that there's always something you could learned about the world.
5.	Memoirs of a Geisha.	Arthur Golden.	Memoic Fiction.	435/!!	Challenging	Dec.	Passage	It's a great book I learned about japanese culture.

Figure 5–2 Students' Reading Log

Name	Dec.	Jan.	Feb.
Student #1	White Hose (F) / The River (F) / The Way Then (F)	Among Friends (F) / Are You There God? It's Me Margaret	Are You There God? It's Me Margaret (F) / Don't Die My Love (O)
Student #2	Go Ask Alice (F) / Real Teens Vol.1 (F) Vol.11 (F)	Treasure love (F)	Geena (F) / Annie's Baby (F)
Student #3	Something Upstairs (A) / Nightmare Hr. (F) / The Babysitter (F)	The Girlfriend (F) / Switched (F)	Blind Date (F) Return? / Heirense (F) Almost Forty?
Student #4	Jay's Journal (F) / Scary Story (F)	The Outsiders (F) / XMas (F)	Switched (A) / That Was Then This Is Now (O) "Goals"
Student #5	White Hose (F) / Go + Come Back (F) / Friends (F) / Switched (F)	Hit & Run (F) Forever (F) / Nightmare Hr. (F) / Twins (F) / Blume (O)	Something Upstairs (F) / Among Friends (F) / Jay's Journal (O)
Student #6	Treasure love (F) / Go Ask Alice (A) / Jay's Journal (F)	→	Last Summer (F) / First Dance (F)
Student #7 Discharge 1/30 (1/1/13)	D.J.S + Mr. Hyde (F) / Frankenstein (F)	Oliver Twist (O)	
		Student #8 →	Dr. Jekyll + Mr. Hyde (F) / Frankenstein (F)

Figure 5–3 Reader's Survey

Reader's Survey

1. How many books have you read from cover to cover this year? __15–25__) 16

2. How many books did you read from cover to cover last year? ____4____

3. What school did you attend last year? __I.H.S__

4. Your reading habits....

	June '00	June '01
a. time spent on reading per week: _3_hrs. x 7 days =	1	3
b. time between books (break btw. books):_O_ days	2	O
c. time it takes you to read an "average" book: _2_ days	4	2

5. Who are you as a reader?...
   a. If you could have given yourself a grade (A,B,C,D,F) to describe yourself as a reader last year, what would you give yourself? __C⁻__ Why? _Because I don't use to like to read book_ Okay, what grade best describes you as a reader now? __B⁺__ Why? _Because Now I give a lot importance to my books. Now I love to read my books._
   b. If you think you have improved as a reader how could you prove it? _I will prove it in the way. If any person ask about the title of the book I still remembered also I can talk about the book._

Using a questionnaire, students were asked to give feedback on the elements of time and choice in the reading program. They were asked to respond to the following questions, "Should we continue to dedicate time to shhhhh! (silent) reading in class? Why?" and "This year you chose the books you wanted to read. What do you think of this idea?" (see Figure 5–4). Another tool used to measure student response was my record of the amount of time students were able to sit and read silently each week during a seventy-minute period.

Figure 5–4 Student Questionnaire

<u>Directions:</u> **Answer the question and brainstorm with your group a list of reasons to support your answer.**

Should we continue to dedicate time to shhhh! reading in class? _yes_
List your reasons:

— Because we spend more time on our books and have more chance to improve our reading.

— Besides, when we read in class we can have the advantage of having a teacher to make any questions clear.

This year you chose the books you wanted to read. What do you think of this idea? _Good_.
List reasons to support your answer:

— Because this way we have more chances to develop any interest on reading books.

— It is also good for teachers because they could get students to read at least a comics book.

Teacher Surveys

The seventy-five students who participated in the reading program are part of a cluster seen by the same group of five teachers throughout the school year. These teachers were asked to comment on students' habits and attitudes toward reading. In addition, I polled a group of high school humanities teachers about the value and reality of providing students with book choice given the school class scheduling and purchasing procedures.

88

Parent Survey

A random sample of the parents of twenty children who took part in the reading class was surveyed about changes in their children's reading habits outside of school (see Figure 5–5).

Figure 5–5 Parent Questionnaire

6/4/01

Dear Parent or Guardian,

     This year at school, the teachers on the PANYC team decided to provide students with an independent reading period two times a week. This meant that Tina was given the opportunity to choose any book from our class library and read it silently in class. We also provided time for students to talk about the books in group or on the computer. We were hoping students would become more excited by reading and better readers by emphasizing reading for pleasure. In addition, we hoped English language skills would improve. Please take a moment to think about Tina's reading habits over this school year - Sept. '00 – June '01 and circle your responses below. If you don't know the response to one of the questions below, please skip it.

1. Spends free time reading : never, less, the same, (more,) a lot more

2. Talks about books: never, less, (the same,) more, a lot more

3. Carries a book around: never, less, the same, (more,) a lot more

4. Buys or requests books: never, (less,) the same, (more,) a lot more

If you have noticed any changes in ~~Mary~~ TINA's reading behavior that you would like to add please tell us below:

We are happy because she
is toying very well and improving
her reading.

Thanks, Carol Tureski
    Reading Teacher/Counselor

Table 5–1 Student Reading Surveys: School Years 1999–2000 and 2000–2001 (n = 75)

Reading Habits	School Year '99–'00	School Year '00–'01
No. of books read	Average: 2 books	Average: 13 books
	Median: 2 books	Median: 9 books
No. of hours spent	Average: 2 hours	Average: 6 hours
reading per week	Median: 1 hour	Median: 7 hours
No. of days spent	Average: 30 days	Average: 3 days
between books	Median: 25 days	Median: 2 days
No. of days spent on	Average: 28 days	Average: 18 days
each book	Median: 25 days	Median: 14 days

Responses

Students read an average of eight more books than they had read the previous year. In addition, students spent more time reading—at least double the amount per week. Students' records showed an improvement in reading speed (see Tables 5–1 and 5–2), as well as interest in more complex books over the course of the year (see Figure 5–1). Most dramatic of all the data collected from students was the change in time between finishing one book and starting another: On the average, students lowered their time between books from thirty to three days (Table 5–1).

Table 5–2 Student Reading Progress: School Year 2000–2001

Indicators of Reading Improvement	Student Records (n = 22)		
	Yes	No	No Response
Student has read books with more pages	18	2	2
Student has read higher-level books	15	5	2
Student has read books of other genres	13	8	1
Student has read books in a shorter time	10	9	3

Student Reflections

One of the main goals of the reading program was to help students find pleasure in reading and perceive themselves as readers. At the beginning of the program, 54 percent of the students assessed themselves as "C" readers, 18 percent as "B" readers, and 4 percent as "A" readers. At the end of the school year, 14 percent graded themselves "C" readers, 54 percent as "B" readers, and 32 percent as "A" readers.

Students were asked to support their grades with explanations. The most common explanation had to do with not having enjoyed reading in the past; however, at the end of the year many wrote of having developed an interest and passion for reading (Figure 5–4). They gave a variety of reasons for their changed perceptions of themselves as readers:

- "I can tell I am a better reader by the difference in books I read before and now, especially the level of the book. I mean I think this year I've read books that are more challenging than last year and much more interesting. Another proof of my improvement is my self-motivation to buy books on my own and experiment."
- "Now I can identify the genre of books that I like to read. Plus, my English is getting better because I know some new words like slam, frigid, smirk, etc."
- "Before I used to read little things, now I read everything I see like newspapers, web pages, and TV stuff—I read from top to bottle (*sic*)."
- "I was a C reader, but now I'm an A reader because now I read books like a computer."
- "Last year I was a C reader because I was reading fine. This year I am an A reader because I eat my books now!"

As the comments above suggest, students liked the idea of choosing their own books. One student commented that she thought it was a great idea to have students choose their own books because if they chose, it would be something they like to read, not something they have to read, and teenagers like to do things they decide to do. They described feeling a sense of importance and responsibility that they associated with making decisions for themselves, and their comments suggested that this feeling motivated them to read more and to read more broadly. One student reasoned that if you like the look of the book, then you'll probably read it.

When asked, "Should we continue to dedicate time in class to silent reading?" the answer from 98 percent was a resounding "Yes." As I pushed to understand their responses, I learned that many of my students did not have time to read at home or had difficulty concentrating on their reading at home. Crowded living conditions, working after school, helping with child care, television—these were the factors that stood in the way of their reading at home. The seventy-minute period gave them an opportunity not available in the rest of their lives to read for an extended period of time and become more engaged with books.

Teacher Reflections

The teachers whom I interviewed saw value in giving students time and choice when it comes to reading, especially in light of our goal to develop students into lifelong learners. They also experienced barriers to supporting students' engagement in reading. Among these were the teachers' limited influence on the design of students' schedules, the lack of extended periods of time with one group of students, and trouble convincing administrators that silent reading in class is part of teaching and is worthwhile. While some had made headway programming for double-period classes in a couple of schools where they observed that students were more engaged in their reading and were reading more, the continuance of these initiatives was not guaranteed.

When I asked the teachers on my team to comment on the impact of the program on our students and themselves, the teachers offered the following:

- "When the reading program was first implemented, I noticed many students had problems holding onto their books, leaving them in the classroom, or on benches in the hallway, and that some did little more than carry them around. However, as the year progressed, it became evident that more students were reading and appeared to be enjoying it. This became clear in one of my classes when students would start to read at the beginning of the period, and I had to tell them to put their books away."

- "What I know is that in my ten years at this high school, I have never seen or heard of so many kids reading so many books. As usual, more girls than boys seem engaged in reading. However, I have had a lot of joy watching many boys deeply engrossed in their reading, as well."

- "I have become aware of students reading who I thought would not be inclined to enjoy reading. Clearly, there were those readers who were avid readers in their native language already, but there were also kids who seemed to catch fire and read more pleasure books in a week than I have read in the last five years."

Parent Reflections

The parents who participated in the reading program surveys wrote that their children were spending more time talking about books and that their children carried books around with them more frequently. Students' requests for books from their parents decreased. Parents attributed this to the fact that their children were getting their reading books at school instead of going to the local library (see Table 5–3).

Table 5–3 Parents' Responses About Children's Reading Habits ($n = 20$)

Student Reading Habits	Never	Less	Same	More	A lot more
Spends free time reading	0%	0%	0%	60%	40%
Talks about book	10%	0%	27%	36%	27%
Carries a book around	0%	10%	0%	63%	27%
Buys or requests books	27%	18%	18%	18%	18%

Some of the comments made by parents to support their observations are as follows:

- "My child has been sleeping less and reading more—most of the time until 1:00 A.M. That makes me proud of my daughter and I need to ask her to stop reading and go to sleep."
- "She likes to read more than watch TV or hang out in the afternoon like before."
- "My daughter has gotten a larger choice of books to read since she started school this year. That's why I think she doesn't go to the public library as much anymore."
- "He likes reading more and he is interested in books. Thanks."

Analysis and Policy Implications

While this is only a small sample, it does suggest that something as simple as changing the schedule to allow our students time to read and providing a range of books had repercussions that went beyond meeting the state standards. As second-language learners, their sense of confidence about their reading grew remarkably. Seeing the students reading more books and reading more quickly suggests to me that their knowledge of the nuances of English improved and that the reading materials they chose were meeting their personal needs as well as helping them to succeed in school. In all likelihood, these changes may have had an impact on the teachers in terms of greater motivation to collaborate and enhanced professionalism. For the families, confidence and pride in their children grew. I am interested in following these students and tracking their level of reading progress as they mature. Further research might focus on the long-term effects of participating in an independent reading program on student achievement.

In terms of policy, this study has a number of implications. In order to promote good literacy practices in the high school, policymakers should consider including teachers in decisions about books and materials selection to ensure meeting the needs of students. In order to accomplish this, the New York City

Board of Education's current book-purchasing system for New York State Text and Library monies should be revamped to allow teachers to purchase books directly from distributors. In order to make informed choices, teachers need to collaborate with colleagues to share their classroom experiences and knowledge. This is clearly a challenge to reshape professional development and rethink the way time is used in school scheduling. If all students are to meet new standards, allocating resources in ways that best serve our students must become our highest priority.

6

Outcomes of Reduced Class Size in High School Math Classrooms

Natasha Warikoo

Natasha Warikoo examines teaching in high school math classes. She makes the case for small class sizes based on her findings that she was teaching better, reaching more students, and receiving more positive feedback from her students. Warikoo found that reduced class size directly impacts the quality of teaching. Her study has implications for policymakers regarding our foci for school reform: resources to meet standards; small class size and conditions of the workplace; peer observations and the status of teaching; professional development based on teachers' needs.

Warikoo shows how a classroom teacher was able to use an impressive range of tools in the course of her everyday teaching. She videotaped a series of classes and analyzed how she spent her time with students. She had peers observe her and made time logs of her class. Additionally, she used student journals, surveys, and interviews. While she set out to look at class size and student achievement, she learned most about her own teaching and changed her teaching practices to accommodate the diverse learners in her classroom.

> I really like this class because there are not a lot of students in class, so that makes it easier for me and other students to learn a lot and more faster.
>
> —Ali, tenth-grade student

*I think this class is better [than last semester's] because there is
not too much students and it easier for me. I mean if there is
too much student it's going to be very noisy to understand math.*
—Habib, tenth-grade student

I began this study with nagging questions: Why are students
more likely to learn a mathematical concept when I sit next to
them and explain it rather than when I elicit a discussion with
the entire class? And, given that this is the case, how can I better
support students in their learning in any class? These questions
led me to wonder, Does class size make a difference in students'
classroom experience? If so, what is it about smaller class size that
helps students, and particularly Limited English Proficient (LEP)
students? Does class size reduction make a difference in LEP high
school algebra students' educational attainment? Because some
studies have shown no educational attainment effects when
teaching methods do not change (Hoxby 2000; Cizek 1999), I
have documented the teaching methods a colleague and I used
and their impact on classes of varying sizes. I also focused on
students' perceptions of the classroom structures that best suited
them.

Review of Literature

I turned to the existing research on the effects of class size reduction. Class size reduction arguments often focus on early
grades; there is little research on the merits of smaller class size
in high school (Finn 1998). Many studies have shown that reducing class size to less than twenty increases student achievement in kindergarten through grade 3 (Krueger 1999; Molnar,
Smith, and Zahorik 1999; Word et al. 1990; Glass and Smith

1978). Tennessee's Project STAR followed students from kindergarten through grade 3 in schools across the state. The study found significant effects of reduced class size on student achievement (Word et al. 1990).

Hoxby (2000) argues that when the size varies from year to year for the same teacher, class size reduction alone will not improve student achievement. She argues that class size reduction will only be effective with concomitant professional development. Cizek (1999) points out that class size reduction does not increase students' one-on-one time with their teachers if teachers do not change their pedagogy. Staff development in conjunction with class size changes maximizes the increases in student achievement made possible by reduced class size. In order to truly take advantage of reduced class sizes, teachers must reflect upon and engage in discussion about how to effectively use their time with a smaller group of students. Wisconsin's Student Achievement Guarantee in Education (SAGE) Project conducted by Molnar and his colleagues (Molnar, Smith, and Zahorik 1999) required reduced-class-size schools to accompany class size reduction with rigorous curricula, increased staff development focused on small class practices, and extended school hours. The benefits of reduced class size will be lost if unqualified or untrained teachers are hired to take on the newly created classes (Pritchard 1999; Finn and Petrilli 1998).

The benefits of class size reduction occur primarily with classes of less than twenty-five students, particularly with classes of less than twenty students (Ellis 1984; Glass and Smith 1978). Wenglinsky (1997) analyzed data from 182 school districts and found that lower student-to-teacher ratios result in higher achievement by improving the school's social environment. Others argue that class size reduction benefits teachers' workloads, not students' experiences (Finn and Petrilli 1998).

Ellis (1984) and Molnar, Smith, and Zahorik (1999) found that at-risk students—economically or educationally disadvantaged students, African American students, and disabled students—tend to benefit even more than the general population from reduced class size. There is a strong argument to be made that class size reduction benefits the neediest students the most (Molnar, Smith, and Zahorik 1999; Word et al. 1990). For example, the SAGE study conducted by Molnar and his colleagues showed that in classes of fifteen students, "African American students gained significantly more than SAGE white students in third grade, closing the achievement gap. . . . In comparison schools, the gap between the performance of white and African American students widened" (4). This closing of the achievement gap is crucial in an educational system where the gap between African American students' performance and white students' performance in mathematics classes generally increases from ages nine to seventeen (Ascher 1983). Even Gregory Cizek (2000), who argued in *Education Week* that the benefits of class size reduction are negligible, wrote in a letter to the editor, "A class of 30 students, none of whom has special needs, may be more effectively taught than a class of 22 students, 12 of whom have identified behavioral, physical, emotional, or cognitive needs" (43). Students feel a greater confidence and friendliness in classrooms with fewer students (Pritchard 1999). If students perceive that their classroom is one in which more learning can take place, then student achievement will increase. This is especially true in mathematics classes, where many students—often girls—experience "math phobia" due to a lack of confidence in their abilities to succeed (American Association of University Women 1992). Thus the psychological effects alone of reduced class size should increase student achievement.

Impact on Teaching

Aside from the most obvious benefit of class size reduction—increased one-on-one time between teachers and individual students—there are other advantages to lower class size that help increase student achievement. Teachers structure their classrooms according to the individual needs of their students; when there are fewer students in a class, there is more individuation. This occurs even when the curriculum is the same for all students; in smaller classes teachers can more closely align the curriculum with the specific needs of students (Molnar, Smith, and Zahorik 1999). Increased classroom order and less time spent on discipline is another benefit of small class size (Molnar, Smith, and Zahorik 1999; Pritchard 1999). Finally, reduced class size makes teaching more manageable and possibly will help to prevent teacher burnout and increase teacher retention (Pritchard 1999).

Heterogeneous grouping in math classes is facilitated by reduced class size. The difficulties of teaching students with diverse math skills have often been cited as a justification for tracking math classes. Detracking our classes so that all students are held to high standards would be more feasible through reduced class size. Teachers can tailor curricula to the needs of individual students, and students can learn from each other (Slavin 1990). Numerous studies have shown that the benefits of tracking to upper-level students are negligible, and the detriments to lower-level students are severe (Slavin 1990; Argys, Rees, and Brewer 1996).

Ellis' (1984) research suggests that classes that focus on skills rather than content are more likely to benefit from class size reduction. English-language learners and students with weak educational foundations will need a focus on basic skills even in high school (Cummins 1981; Garcia 2000; Krashen 1981a). Thus, students with weak or minimal educational backgrounds in English may benefit from class size reduction even in the upper grades. Resnick (1988) and Lampert (1986) argue for mathematics as an "ill-structured discipline" in which students develop "more meaningful, flexible, and inventive problem solving," and teachers act as coaches in students' development of ideas about mathematics.

Context and Method

The research site, Manhattan International High School (MIHS), admits only recently arrived immigrants who are classified as English-language learners. The school operates on the Coalition of Essential Schools model, maintaining an enrollment of three hundred students and twenty teachers. A coordinating council with teacher, student, parent, and administrative representatives makes all major decisions regarding the school's operation. Teachers write the school's curricula, and frequently employ cooperative learning and student-centered pedagogies. Classes last for seventy minutes. At the time of this writing, students graduate by presenting a portfolio of original work to a panel of teachers; however, the state of New York has required MIHS to end the portfolio process and replace it with Regents examinations as the graduation requirement. The new requirement is being phased in over the next few years.

Student-centered work is at the heart of Manhattan International High School's pedagogy. Students perform such tasks as small-group problem solving, group projects, and individual practice problems. Students always discuss material and help each other understand the mathematical concepts in class, even when they are working on individual practice problems. During the 1999–2000 school year, I taught algebra classes of fifteen and twenty students each. Both classes contained a mix of ninth- and tenth-grade students. These two classes provided for a natural comparison of pedagogy, student experiences, and student performance in classes of different sizes but with the same teacher and school. Both classes are small in comparison to most New York City public school classrooms. However, one is obviously smaller than the other, and I thought a comparison of the two could help me to understand the impact of class size reduction.

What I Learned About Reduced Class Size

To study the impact of reduced class size on my students I used class videos, peer observations, student journals, student interviews, and student surveys.

Class Videos and Peer Observations

I videotaped a series of classes—mine and a colleague's—and later analyzed the use of time in our math classes. Also, my peers observed me and made time logs of my class. I did the same for one peer who teaches math in a style similar to my own with twenty-five students. We discussed the differences in our classes and determined which instructional patterns may have been caused by the different class sizes.

Figure 6–1 shows the use of time in five typical class periods, with class sizes ranging from twelve to twenty-four students. Shaded areas indicate times in which students worked in groups. On the four days that I documented my use of time, students worked in groups for an average of thirty-eight minutes per session—fifty-five percent of the time. My colleague's class worked in groups fifty out of the seventy minutes on the day documented.

As Figure 6–1 shows, a typical lesson in a seventy-minute math class involves whole class discussion and student work time. Often the schedule is as follows:

- *Whole-class discussion*—Attendance, review of homework, introduction and discussion of a new topic including vocabulary for that topic, and asking students what they know about a new topic.
- *Group work*—Practice problems done at tables of three to five students, group task performed at table to be presented later to entire class, and semantic map assignments in groups. During this time, the teacher circulates and assists either individuals or groups with the task at hand.
- *Whole-class discussion*—Wrap-up of the task just completed, student presentations, and homework explanation.

Student Journals

The journals provided me with an initial understanding of my students' perceptions of their learning styles in math class. I asked the students the following questions:

1. Think about how you learn in math class. What is the easiest way for you to learn math: Small group work with your peers? One-on-one explanations with your teacher? Class discussions and explanations by your teacher?

Figure 6–1 Use of Time in Five Typical Math Classes

	Homework check, explanation	Introductory group activity: semantic maps	Introduction to lesson, homework review	Introduction to lesson, homework review	Introduction to lesson; class discussion of new concepts
0–5 mins	Homework check, explanation	Introductory group activity: semantic maps	Introduction to lesson, homework review	Introduction to lesson, homework review	Introduction to lesson; class discussion of new concepts
5–10 mins		Class discussion on semantic maps and new material			
10–15 mins			Group problem-solving	Students do problems on board	Group activity
15–20 min					
20–25 mins	Classwork in groups	Students work on a problem with help of group members	Class review of group problem; each group assigned 1 problem to solve and present to class	Class review of new material	
25–30 mins			Groups work on problem together	Students work at tables on problems	
30–35 mins					
35–40 mins					Teacher explains activity to class
40–45 mins			Groups put solutions on board, then explain their answers to the class; I add to their explanations		Students work on practice problems in groups
45–50 mins					
50–55 mins		Class reviews problem together			
55–60 mins		Students work on more problems			
60–65 mins				I explain common problems I noticed in students' work during groupwork to whole class	
65–70 mins		Class reviews one problem	Homework explanation		Wrap-up of lesson

Note: Shaded areas indicate small group work.

2. Do you pay attention when we have whole-class discussions?
3. What helps you or prevents you from paying attention when we review problems as a class?
4. What changes in the class structure would help you improve in math class?
5. Compare your class this semester to your class last semester. How are the classes different? Do you find it easier or more difficult to learn this semester? Explain your answer.
6. With whom should you sit so you can learn most effectively?

In their journals, students wrote of their appreciation for the time we spend reviewing problems as a class. One student said that in math class he likes to work on group and class discussions and my explanations, because in these ways it's easier for him to learn math. In group, he could discuss with others and in class discussion he could learn many things that he didn't understand.

In response to my request that the class describe two helpful things about the day's class one student wrote, "It's quiet in the room—that helps me concentrate. We help each other with the difficult parts. We understand better."

Student Surveys

I developed a survey to see if there were similarities in my students' experiences of algebra class. I asked them about the most valuable time during math class, when they were able to concentrate best, and how this year's class compared to last year's. I also asked, how much time does the teacher spend with you during math class? I gave them a range of zero to fifteen minutes. I ended the questionnaire by asking, "Would you prefer that our math class have more students, fewer students, or the same number of students."

In reviewing my data from surveys, I discovered recurring themes related to time, concentration, and teaching methods.

Figure 6–2 Graph of Student Response to Survey Questions

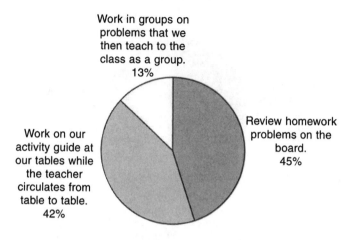

The most valuable time during math class
is when we . . .

Work in groups on
problems that we
then teach to the
class as a group.
13%

Work on our
activity guide at
our tables while
the teacher
circulates from
table to table.
42%

Review homework
problems on the
board.
45%

According to survey responses, students appreciated the time we spent on reviewing problems as a class (see Figure 6–2). When asked when they concentrate most during math class, forty-four percent of students responded, "When the teacher sits next to me and explains a problem." They reported concentrating more during individual time with the teacher than when working independently (see Figure 6–3).

Student Interviews

Student interviews gave me an opportunity to really understand how students felt about their learning process in math class, beyond what they wrote in their journals. I asked:

1. In which part of math class do you feel you learn the most, and why? (Class discussion? Group work while teacher circulates? Group presentations? Homework? Tests? Journals?)

Figure 6–3 Survey Responses Showing Students' Best Concentration

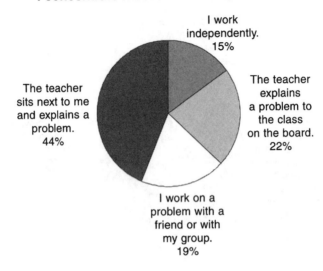

I concentrate most in math class when . . .

I work
independently.
15%

The teacher
explains
a problem to
the class
on the board.
22%

I work on a
problem with a
friend or with
my group.
19%

The teacher
sits next to me
and explains a
problem.
44%

2. About how much time does the teacher spend with you, on average, during every class? Is this enough? How does this compare to your other classes? How does this compare to your previous math classes?
3. We have X number of students in our class. Would you prefer that size increase, decrease, or stay the same? Explain your answer.
4. Are you doing better, worse, or the same in math class compared to last semester (and last year)? Can you explain the difference, if there's a difference?
5. What motivates and/or encourages you to concentrate and think hard during math class?
6. What helps or prevents you from following class discussions? How could class discussions be restructured to help you get more out of them?

In journals and interviews, many students echoed the sentiments of one student who said that in his other school [the junior high school] the students didn't pay attention to the teacher . . . they talked or did whatever they wanted . . . the teacher couldn't tell which students understood. In larger classes, these students reported that other students' questions made lectures confusing and hard to follow—that is, the more questions asked, the fewer the students who could follow the teacher's explanation.

Many students wanted the smallest class size possible. For them, fewer students are always better. Some students found it difficult to concentrate when their classes of fifteen to twenty students were "too noisy." In smaller classes, less noise enabled students to help one another. One student said that she learns quickly when one person explains, but cannot learn when everyone talks at the same time. She later suggested that when the classroom is crowded it becomes loud, and everyone needs help, so covering material takes longer: "Sometimes it's too noisy. It's so noisy, I can't think of anything. The more students the noisier it is, I can't learn like that."

Students appreciated their small classes during cooperative learning not only because they could work with their peers but also because the teacher had more time to spend with them individually. One student said that while working together in groups, if you don't understand you are able to ask. Many others expressed similar sentiments. When asked what helped him during class, another student said that the most helpful thing that he had was a friend; that his friend helped him to learn more and to understand better.

Analysis

The videotapes and observations revealed some interesting information about the way teachers and students interact. I watched my colleague circulate among the students in her geometry class as they worked on a task together and noticed that she worked with groups of students rather than with individuals. I analyzed the videos of my classroom for my movement patterns.

Figure 6–4 Graph of Teacher Time Spent with Students

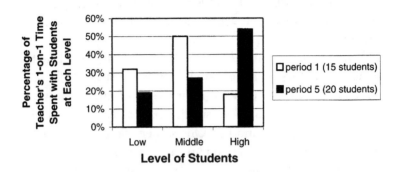

**Percent of Teacher's Time with Students
of Different Academic Levels**

Using student grades from the first and second quarters, I split students roughly into three categories: low achieving (twenty-five percent), middle achieving (fifty percent), and high achieving (twenty-five percent) (see Figure 6–4). Then, I used time logs from eight class videotapes and peer observations of my teaching to determine how much time I spent with students in all three categories. I found that students who perform in the middle fifty percent of their math class tended to participate most in class discussions. Also, I found that in my class of twenty students, I spent more time during classwork with high achieving students than with low achieving students. In the class of fifteen students, this trend reversed.

This result appears in spite of the fact that I often take note of which students I have and have not worked with during a class period. In a larger class, it is more likely that the most confident and outspoken students will receive the most attention from me.

Other benefits of reduced class size emerged from the journals, surveys, and interviews of students at MIHS. Quieter classrooms with fewer distractions enabled them to concentrate better. There were increased interactions among students and one-on-

one time with teachers; improved cooperative learning; and increased attention paid to low-achieving students.

Judging from the student responses, fewer students means more time with the teacher. For students, this one-on-one time with the teacher may be the most valuable few minutes they spend in class every day. With class size reduction, teachers can devote more time to individual students during class time. They can also design individualized curricula for their students. Reduced class size also facilitates cooperative learning by making the teacher more available for group consultation.

Reducing class size makes heterogeneity within the class manageable. Often I assigned different assignments to students depending on their prior knowledge of the material they were studying. In my class of fifteen students, I had students who still struggled with fractions alongside students who could graph and analyze quadratic equations. Cooperative learning, leveled lessons, and extra credit assignments addressed this diversity. Imagine the larger range and increased variation necessary in a larger heterogeneous class.

I also found that my observations of colleagues as well as colleagues' observations of my own teaching sparked changes in my teaching, ranging from better blackboard usage, to lessons paced differently, to recognizing the needs of particular students whom I had overlooked.

Policy Recommendations

The two policy recommendations that emerge from my research are:

- Implement class size reduction in all schools.
- Provide professional development to support teachers' learning the most effective methods to maximize the benefits of small class sizes.

Given the result that reduced class size made me more attentive to the lowest-achieving students, I recommend policies emphasizing reduced class size for the most troubled schools as well as for Limited English Proficient students. To raise standards for all students including those who struggle with the most basic skills, class size must be sufficiently small to ensure that all students get the proper attention from their teachers.

Reduced class size will be most beneficial when accompanied by ongoing professional development on effective use of class size reduction. Professional development should include teachers' participation through reflection and discussion and peer mentoring, in which colleagues in the same school become critical friends by observing in each other's classrooms on a regular basis. Professional development that supports reduced class size should also focus on time management, cooperative learning, reduced lecture time, teaching to a heterogeneous class, and identifying individual students' needs.

Finally, time and support built into teachers' schedules to do action research in their classrooms will result in better teaching. Action research, the process by which this paper was done, resulted in positive changes in my teaching. For example, I became more aware of the time I spent with individual students, so that more students could benefit from my time spent circulating from table to table during group work. Consequently, I did periodic time logs of my teaching to examine how I spent time with individual students during class. Also, I made my classes more formally structured with direct teacher instruction after students' journals and survey responses indicated that they appreciated lecture time in class.

Class size reduction, given its large costs, powerful effects, and mixed research results, will continue to be hotly debated in education policy. This study provides one glimpse into the benefits of class size reduction for the high school Limited English Proficient student, both from the student's perspective as well as through objective measures of time spent in the classroom. Unfortunately, the study's length and scale did not permit an analysis of specific student achievement results. Because the two classes closely studied are both small by the standards of New

York City public high schools, and the classes also benefit from other aspects of MIHS, such as being a small school and having democratic governance and portfolio assessment, it is impossible to speak conclusively as to whether student achievement resulted from reduced class size or from a myriad of other aspects of the school.

Appendix A: Questions for Student Journals

1. Think about how you learn in math class. What is the easiest way for you to learn math—small-group work with your peers? one-on-one explanations with your teacher? class discussions and explanations by your teacher?
2. Do you pay attention when we have whole-class discussions?
3. What helps you or prevents you from paying attention when we review problems as a class?
4. What changes in the class structure would help you improve in math class?
5. Compare your class this semester to your class last semester. How are the classes different? Do you find it easier or more difficult to learn this semester? Explain your answer.
6. With whom should you sit so you can learn most effectively?

Appendix B: Student Interview Questions

1. In which part of math class do you feel you learn the most, and why? (Class discussion? Group work while teacher circulates? Group presentations? Homework? Tests? Journals?)
2. About how much time does the teacher spend with you, on average, during every class? Is this enough? How does this compare to your other classes? to your previous math classes?
3. We have X number of students in our class. Would you prefer that size increase, decrease, or stay the same? Explain your answer.

4. Are you doing better, worse, or the same in math class compared to last semester (and last year)? Can you explain the difference, if there's a difference?
5. What motivates (encourages) you to concentrate and think hard during math class?
6. What helps or prevents you from following class discussions? How could they be restructured to help you get more out of them?

Appendix C: Student Survey

Name (Optional):

CLASS SURVEY QUESTIONS: choose one answer for each question.

1. The most valuable time during math class is when we:
   (a) Review homework problems on the board
   (b) Work on our activity guide at our tables while the teacher circulates (moves) from table to table
   (c) Work in groups on problems that we then teach to the class as a group
2. I concentrate most in math class when:
   (a) I work independently (by myself)
   (b) The teacher explains a problem to the class on the board
   (c) I work on a problem with a friend or with my group
   (d) The teacher sits next to me and explains a problem
3. Compared to last semester, my grades in math class are:
   (a) Better
   (b) Worse
   (c) The same
   Explain why.
4. About how much time does the teacher spend with you during math class?
   (a) 0–5 minutes
   (b) 5–10 minutes
   (c) 10–15 minutes
   (d) More than 15 minutes

5. Would you prefer that our math class have:
   (a) More students
   (b) Fewer students
   (c) The same number of students
   Explain why.

7

The Empire State Strikes Back
Portfolio Culture in the Regents Era

Janet Ruth Price

Janet Price combines two studies she conducted in 1999 and 2001 to take on one of the most controversial topics in education—high-stakes standardized testing versus multiple forms of assessment. Price teaches at a New York City public high school designed for non-English-speaking students who have been in this country for less than four years. The school implemented a portfolio assessment system that clearly raised levels of teaching practice and student achievement but has lost the state assessment battle to on-demand testing. Her study exposes the fault line between a school's responsibility to best educate its specific student population and the policies that require standardization in teaching and assessment.

Price buttresses her argument with data that examines student work over a three-year period in two different curriculum areas—social studies and science. She also documents the difference in student performance on similar tasks in the on-demand situation of the test and in the context of classroom assignments. Analysis of student work is the central focus of this study. Price shows us how powerful it can be. ♥

This paper is a composite of two studies examining the tension between performance assessment and on-demand testing. The first study, completed in 1999, focuses on International High School's assessment system, which requires every senior to complete and present a portfolio of specified "Performance Based Assessment Tasks" (PBATs). This system was begun during the 1995–96 school year under a special five-year variance from the state's competency testing program. I questioned whether later portfolios would demonstrate a higher achievement level than earlier ones because of the ongoing work of the faculty to align both curriculum and assessment to state standards and to clarify the criteria for judging student portfolios. To answer my question, I compared work from earlier and later portfolios.

During the variance period, a new statewide policy was implemented requiring all public high school graduates to pass five Regents exams. (Previously, the more difficult Regents were not a requirement for a local high school diploma.) Pursuant to this new policy, the New York State Education Department declined to renew the variance and, beginning in the 2000–01 school year, our seniors were required to pass the Regents English Language Arts (ELA) exam. The second study compares student work on that exam to student work on comparable tasks undertaken as classroom assignments. In this case the question was: How do students respond to similar tasks in dissimilar contexts?

I will begin by describing the context for the two studies— the school's effort over the past seven years first to develop the graduation portfolio process and, more recently, to save it. Next I will describe my research methodologies and then report and analyze my findings. I will use changes in my own classroom practice to illustrate how development and implementation of portfolio rubrics can be effective professional development. Finally, I discuss the policy implications of these findings for my school, the city, state, and beyond.

Context

International High School (IHS) at LaGuardia Community College admits only students from non-English-speaking countries who have been in this country for less than four years. In its fourteen years, this small school of 450 students has been a laboratory for innovation, including piloting the school-based option, now available in the union contract, for a faculty personnel committee responsible for hiring teachers.

Since the school began piloting its graduation portfolio system in 1995–96, large amounts of time and effort have been expended to align our curriculum with state standards; refine our system of performance-based assessment; and familiarize teachers, students, and parents with what is expected in a graduation portfolio. To demonstrate the steps necessary to implement such a system, a brief chronology follows.

1995–96: First Steps

In the first year of the pilot, the school operated under a mixed system since many students had already taken and passed the Regents Competency Tests (RCT). For students who had not passed all the RCTs, the portfolio simply supplemented their RCT results. General criteria for judging portfolios were an early work product of the International Partnership, the network of the three International High Schools in Queens, Brooklyn, and Manhattan (and one of the first school networks in the Annenberg-sponsored New York Networks for School Renewal). The partnership criteria focused on what habits of mind should be reflected in presentations of student work.

1996–97: Standardization of the Portfolio Presentation

For the next year, 1996–97, my first in the IHS community, the partnership statement was supplemented with clearer guidelines for the kind of work to include in the graduation portfolio and how to constitute the graduation certification panels. Time for this work was allocated at a weekend retreat with representatives from all three schools, on staff development days that brought together the faculties of all three schools, at monthly school faculty meetings, and during weekly instructional team meetings. Faculty was organized in interdisciplinary instructional teams, each serving a heterogeneous group of about seventy-five students in all four grades. Beginning in the 2000–01 year the teams were reconfigured to serve either ninth and tenth graders or eleventh and twelfth graders. What would qualify as appropriate work was still largely left to teachers and certification panel members.

Among the accomplishments of the 1996–97 year were:

- a common list and definitions of the "Performance Based Assessment Tasks" (PBATs) that would be required in graduation portfolios for the three schools
- an alignment of those tasks with the state content standards in math, science, English, and social studies—that is, an analysis of what kinds of content mastery a particular PBAT could demonstrate
- a review of samples of student work from the three schools, including some that had been presented in graduation portfolios, comparing them to the state content standards and discussing "how good is good enough"
- an analysis by each of the interdisciplinary instructional teams of how its curriculum aligned with the state content standards
- some revisions of curriculum to better align students' learning opportunities with the state content standards
- participation by faculty at the three International High Schools on each other's graduation portfolio panels, which not only made the panels more accountable but also facilitated development of a common understanding of how such panels should be conducted and contributed to the development of common standards for student work

In the summer of 1997, draft rubrics were developed for each "Performance Based Assessment Task," drawing heavily on state subject-area standards and New Standards Project materials, specifying a number of criteria for each PBAT, and describing outstanding, passing, and unsatisfactory performance for each such criterion.

1997–99: Refining and Applying the International Rubrics

Since the 1997–98 school year, rubrics have been in place to determine whether senior portfolios meet graduation standards.

117

For this system to be both fair and effective, the rubrics first created in the summer of 1997 were tested on student work and refined to improve interrater agreement. Parents and teachers had to be informed of specific standards for graduation portfolio work. Teachers had to adjust their assignments and classroom strategies to ensure that students, especially seniors, produced appropriate work for the graduation portfolio. Faculty and team meetings as well as partnership meetings were dominated by these activities. A curriculum committee produced a set of documents to clarify what is expected of students, their faculty mentors, and the graduation certification panels, including handbooks specifically prepared for students and parents.

Meeting the Challenge of the New Regents Exams

In 1997, the New York State Board of Regents decided to phase out the Regents Competency Tests and phase in a universal set of new Regents exams. With encouragement from the New York City Board of Education, the schools operating under the variance from the RCTs formed the New York Performance Standards Consortium to develop a common graduation-by-portfolio system aligned with state standards. The consortium sought endorsement from the state of this system as an alternative to the new Regents. The graduation portfolio would continue to include a research paper, literary essay, math project, science project, and on-demand oral presentation before a certification panel, as well as other tasks determined by the individual school. Over thirty schools citywide participated in the effort to create a performance-based portfolio alternative to the Regents exams.

Facing the Reality of a Mixed System

In April 2001, the state education commissioner formally rejected the consortium's proposal. He made this decision despite the recommendation to extend the variance for another three years, a recommendation made by the "Blue Ribbon Panel" that he himself had appointed to evaluate the results of the original variance. He did, however, give consortium schools some extra time to phase in the Regents exams. Beginning with the class of 2005, all five Regents exams will be required. However, students in earlier cohorts will be required only to pass the ELA exam.

IHS administered the ELA Regents for the first time in 2000–01. For now, IHS, like most of the consortium schools, is continuing to graduate students by portfolio. A trial court decision upholding the denial of the variance is now under appeal. If the state prevails, students will begin taking other Regents exams during the 2002–03 school year. IHS and other consortium schools will scramble for ways to preserve performance-based assessment as on-demand testing pressures increase.

Method

Study One

Has student work included in portfolios improved since the inception of the portfolio system?

I wondered whether setting standards for PBATs at the school level would result in changes in classroom practice, including more rigorous assignments and more targeted help that would, in turn, lead to improved student work. To see whether the development of the performance assessment system has had a positive effect on student performance by helping students meet state standards, I decided to examine and compare student work across the first three years of portfolio assessment. I focused on students in the middle of their respective class rankings on the theory that their work was more likely to be affected by teacher intervention and schoolwide changes than that of the highest- or lowest-performing students.

On file in my school are portfolios for all graduates. A student intern selected portfolios from 1997, 1998, and 1999, keeping only the portfolios of students whose grade-point average placed them in the middle of their class ranking. No work produced in my class was included in the sample.

I decided to focus on two specific PBATs, the social studies research paper and the science project or experiment. Since I teach social studies and assign at least one research paper per year, I felt that a close examination of the papers assigned by other teachers would help me understand how the rubric criteria were shaping our practice. I also wanted to look at a PBAT in a subject I do not teach. I chose the science project in part because, like the research paper, it is supposed to be organized around a central question, thesis, or hypothesis. Also, some concern had been expressed in my school about the rigor of the science work in students' portfolios. I, therefore, thought it would be helpful to see if, in fact, we were making progress in improving that rigor.

In order to compare papers, I needed to apply the same criteria for each paper. The performance rubrics provided relevant criteria and descriptions of various levels of achievement for each standard. However, rather than use the internally developed PBAT rubrics now being used at my school, I opted to apply the draft rubrics recently developed by the New York Performance Standards Consortium (see Figures 7–1, 7–2). These rubrics were drafted in the fall of 1998, refined through moderation studies, and were ready for wider testing to ensure adequate interrater agreement. They include similar performance indicators to those already in place at IHS, but with somewhat more detailed descriptions of what constitutes outstanding, good, passing, and insufficient performance. Since these rubrics would eventually supersede those in use in my school, and since they represent the best thinking of a wide group of educators, I was eager to work with them. It also made sense to use externally developed criteria to evaluate the effectiveness of our internally developed assessment system, not merely to measure student achievement but also to think about how to improve it.

My primary data is, thus, student work. However, to understand the nexus between creation of the rubrics in 1997 and changes in subsequent graduation portfolio projects, I also conducted two informal discussions with social studies and science teachers in groups of three or four. I asked three questions:

Figure 7–1 New York Performance Standards Consortium Assessment Rubric

NEW YORK PERFORMANCE STANDARDS CONSORTIUM
SCIENCE EXPERIMENT/PROJECT
Extended Project or Original Experiment

Performance Indicator	OUTSTANDING	GOOD	COMPETENT	NEEDS REVISION
Problem to be Investigated	Hypothesis or thesis is testable and thoughtful and/or original. Background information is researched in several sources, including at least one scientific journal. Hypothesis or thesis reflects a synthesis of the primary background research.	Hypothesis or thesis is testable and thoughtful. Background information is researched in several sources, including at least one scientific journal. Hypothesis or thesis reflects an understanding of the background research.	Hypothesis or thesis is testable. Background information is researched in several popular sources. Hypothesis or thesis reflects basic understanding of the background research.	Does not have a hypothesis or thesis. Background information is researched in one source. Hypothesis or thesis does not reflect an understanding of the research.
Experimental Design/Project Design	Appropriately identifies and describes all variables in the experiment or project. Uses accepted or appropriate technology and tools to gather and analyze data, and recognizes bias in data collection.	Appropriately identifies and describes most of the variables in the experiment or project. Uses accepted or appropriate technology and tools to gather and analyze data.	Appropriately identifies and describes some of the variables in the experiment or project. Uses technology and tools to gather and analyze data.	Appropriately identifies and describes one of the variables in the experiment or project. Does not use appropriate technology and tools to gather and analyze data.
Results	Number of trials or depth of research is extremely thorough. Uses basic algebraic functions and more than one statistical test for data analysis. Creates graphs and charts which reflect the use of basic algebraic functions and multiple statistical tests. Makes clear and meticulous observations.	Number of trials or depth of research is thorough. Uses basic algebraic functions and a statistical test for data analysis. Creates graphs and charts which reflect the use of basic algebraic functions and a statistical test. Makes clear observations.	Number of trials or depth of research is adequate. Uses basic algebraic functions for data analysis. Creates graphs and charts which reflect the use of basic algebraic functions. Makes adequate observations.	Number of trials or depth of research is not adequate. Does not use mathematical procedures during data analysis. Creates graphs and charts which do not reflect the proper use of mathematical procedures. Does not make adequate observations.
Analysis of Results	Creatively interprets hypothesis in light of results. Poses creative questions to explore further. Recognizes the moral, social, aesthetic and/or environmental implications of the experiment.	Thoughtfully interprets hypothesis in light of results. Poses thoughtful questions to explore further. Recognizes more than one connection of the experiment to a larger context.	Adequately interprets hypothesis in light of results. Poses adequate questions to explore further. Recognizes a connection of the experiment to a larger context.	Does not interpret hypothesis as related to results. Does not pose questions to explore further. Does not recognize a connection of the experiment to a larger context.
Presentation	Thoroughly answers questions relevant to the experiment and related topics. Makes imaginative use of multimedia to display and represent the experiment (e.g., computer models, poster board, slide show, videos, art work, music, etc.)	Adequately answers questions relevant to the experiment and related topics. Uses multimedia to display and represent the experiment (e.g., computer models, poster board, videos, art work, music, etc.)	Adequately answers questions relevant to the experiment. Uses one type of media to display and represent the experiment (e.g., computer models, poster board, slide show, videos, art work, music, etc.)	Does not adequately answer questions relevant to the experiment. Does not use multimedia to display and represent the experiment.

Figure 7–2 New York Performance Standards Consortium Social Studies Research Paper

RESEARCH PAPER: Write, revise and present an original research paper

Performance Indicators	OUTSTANDING	GOOD	COMPETENT	NEEDS REVISION
Effective and appropriate use of evidence	Detailed evidence drawn mainly from primary sources Evaluation of substantial number of opposing/varied sources Effective analysis of all sources	Some evidence drawn from primary sources Evaluation of some opposing or varied sources Works thoroughly with all sources	Adequate use of primary sources Adequate use of opposing/varied sources Refers to and analyzes several available sources	Inadequate use/absence of primary sources No variation in types, opinions, or perspectives of resources
Effective Organization	Has clearly defined organizing idea, thesis or question Complex argument clearly presented and supported by specific and relevant evidence: explanation of why opposing arguments are less valid Clear, compelling introduction: conclusion that effectively synthesizes the strands of its main argument. All aspects of the paper support the overall structure. Clear, effective transition in which ideas flow logically from each other	Has clearly defined organizing idea, thesis, or questions Clear introduction and well constructed thoughtful conclusion. Most aspects of the paper support the overall structure. Clear transitions. Presentation of clear argument supported by reasonable evidence: some opposing arguments countered but not all	Organizing idea may be too broad or ill-defined, but present. Transitions may be abrupt or minimal but reader generally follows Evidence not clearly connected at the organizing idea but the reader is able to make the connection	No stated organizing idea. Paper disjointed, unfocused. No discernable introduction or conclusion Evidence may be present but does not support any particular idea.
Understanding of connections	Demonstrate relation between main idea and larger context Analysis of issues yield well developed, original ideas and new understanding	Recognizes patterns and can make accurate generalizations Explains and applies the relationship between concepts and issues beyond the work	Ideas are presented clearly and logically Connections to a larger context are not explicit but implies such connections could be made	No connections made to a larger context Shows no understanding of student knowledge or development of new ideas
Strong, well expressed viewpoint (student voice)	Confident writing style: student voice is evident writes with lively, engaging language Paper has distinct, individual identity	Writing is clear and focused: style is straight-forward but not original Student voice is present but inconsistent	Writing is generally clear	Writing is unclear with no particular style, individuality or student voice
Conventions	Grammar and punctuation are nearly flawless: appropriate documentation of sources (bibliography and citations). Use quotations and paraphrasing to sustain an argument.	Some grammar and punctuation errors but writing is solid overall: appropriate documentation of sources. Uses quotations and paraphrasing to sustain an argument	Some grammar and punctuation errors but does not impact understanding of content Sources are correctly documented though occasional errors in paraphrasing and quotations	Grammar and punctuation errors interfere with understanding of content Sources used not documented consistently or documented incorrectly
External Assessment and Validation	Communicates clear message in appropriate, sophisticated and original way to audience Present complex, accurate, substantive information and ideas in an organized way Answers questions accurately, thoughtfully and effectively and makes larger connections	Communicates clear message in appropriate and knowledgeable way to audience. Presents substantive, accurate information in an organized way Answers questions accurately, thoughtfully and effectively	Communicates clear message in appropriate way to audience Presents some substantive, accurate information in an organized way Answers questions accurately and effectively	Message is not clear or appropriate to audience Does not present accurate or substantive information or ideas are not organized Unable to answer questions accurately or effectively

- How have you changed your projects to better fit the rubrics?
- How have you changed your schedules, curriculum, and use of classroom time to fit in the more challenging projects?
- What do science and social studies teachers have in common in this regard?

Some teachers were able to produce samples of the written instructions they gave to students before the rubrics were in place and after. The graduation portfolios yielded many examples of "before" and "after" student projects based on these instructions. I have focused on the changes in two specific projects that appear frequently in students' portfolios in all three years—a science project based on keeping plant logs and a research project on the Bill of Rights. I also describe how I have changed the research projects I assign in response not only to the rubrics themselves, but also as a result of discussions with other teachers.

I knew from my own experience that since the rubrics were first introduced in the fall of 1997, the school has provided a variety of opportunities for teachers to meet to discuss their implementation. It is reasonable to expect that these professional development opportunities affected teacher practice. They certainly affected my practice. Therefore, I reviewed school meeting agendas and my own teaching journal to document what the faculty as a whole has done over the past four years to align both curriculum and assessment to state standards and to clarify the criteria for judging student portfolios.

Finally, I was curious as to whether our students were aware of the criteria for projects embodied in the rubrics. I took the opportunity to survey my own class of twenty-four students before they embarked on their first social studies research paper of the year. Specifically, I asked them to list the five most important characteristics of a good research paper. My guess was that students new to the school would have very different answers from students who had been in the school at least two years.

Study Two

How do students respond to similar tasks in dissimilar contexts?

When the January 2001 Regents ELA exam was administered at IHS, I noticed that one section, "Reading and Writing for Literary Response," was similar in format to an assignment I give to my students every spring. In both cases, students read two pieces of literature and write a literary essay on a topic suggested by the pieces, using the pieces to develop their ideas.

In the case of the January Regents, the two readings were descriptive narratives, one about a thunderstorm, and the other about an airplane show. The instructions were: "Write a unified essay about the discovery of beauty. In your essay, use ideas from both passages to establish a controlling idea about the discovery of beauty. Using evidence from each passage, develop your controlling idea, and show how the author uses specific literary elements or techniques to convey that idea." Those are the standard instructions for that section of the ELA; the only variation in the administration of the test is the readings and the essay topic.

My classroom assignment was part of a semester-long exploration of the African American experience in history and literature. Students read poetry of the Harlem Renaissance and chose two poems on which to base an essay exploring the effect of discrimination on a person's sense of self and their place in the world.

After the January Regents were scored, I looked at the test booklets of a student who had failed the Regents, a student who had narrowly passed the test, and a student who had comfortably passed. The school is required to keep students' Regents test booklets on file. I was able to read students' test responses and to see their scores on different parts of the exam. Since this was the first time we had administered the ELA Regents at our school, I was curious to know how the students felt about this test. On the first day of the new semester, I gave students time to do freewriting about what they liked or disliked about the test format, how they thought they had done, and how they felt about passing or failing.

In June, when my three target students turned in their Harlem Renaissance assignments, I copied their work before returning it. I was able to compare student work produced in two very different situations. I used the rubrics developed for scoring this part of the Regents exam and compared how students met the five criteria of the rubrics in the two writing samples. I also used the freewrites done soon after the test as evidence of the impact of the test both on students who passed it and those who did not.

Findings

Study One

In my quest to determine whether student work improved with portfolio assessment, I organized my data in two sets of tables. My evaluation of research papers is presented in Tables 7–1, 7–2, and 7–3. My evaluation of the science papers is presented in Tables 7–4, 7–5, and 7–6. Both sets of tables are organized by performance indicator and score as determined by the rubrics developed by the New York Performance Standards Consortium. Students are identified by their year and class rank. For each PBAT, I evaluate several samples of student work across the three years and explain why I scored the paper as I did.

Discussion

Only one of the ten 1997 papers (the baseline data) passed every criteria. Three of the ten papers lacked even the most rudimentary citations or bibliographies, making it impossible to discern what sources were used for the alleged research. Eight of the ten papers had no discernable thesis and/or did not make adequate use of evidence such as primary sources or current scholarship. For example, one paper was titled "Why Do All Americans Remember and Honor Thomas Jefferson?" The writer relies on two encyclopedia entries, two recent books about Thomas Jefferson, and unspecified Internet information resulting in a report comprised of biographical facts and a list of major accomplishments. There are no opposing or varied viewpoints

Table 7–1 Results of Analysis of Social Studies Research Papers in 1997 Graduation Portfolios

Rubric Criteria	Rank									
	44	46	50	56	59	60	65	69	71	85
Use of Evidence	C	NR	NR	C	C	NR	NR	NR	NR	NR
Thesis/Organization	C	NR	C	NR	C	C	NR	NR	C	NR
Making Connections	C	G	C	C	C	G	C	C	G	C
Voice and Style	C	C	C	C	C	G	C	C	G	C
Use of Conventions	NR	C	C	C	C	G	C	C	NR	NR

E = Excellent; G = Good; C = Competent (passing); NR = Needs Revision (does not pass the rubric).

Table 7–2 Results of Analysis of Social Studies Research Papers in 1998 Graduation Portfolios

Rubric Criteria	Rank							
	38	50	56	61	64	68	72	75
Use of Evidence	C	G	G	C	C	C	C	C
Thesis/Organization	NR	G	G	G	G	G	C	C
Making Connections	G	G	C	G	G	C	C	C
Voice and Style	G	G	C	G	C	C	C	C
Use of Conventions	G	G	G	G	C	C	NR	C

E = Excellent; G = Good; C = Competent (passing); NR = Needs Revision (does not pass the rubric).

Table 7–3 Results of Analysis of Social Studies Research Papers in 1999 Graduation Portfolios

Rubric Criteria	Rank									
	49	54	56	57	70	72	77	79	83	85
Use of Evidence	C	G	C	O	G	C	C	G	E	O
Thesis/Organization	C	G	C	O	O	NR	C	O	O	O
Making Connections	G	G	G	O	C	C	G	O	O	G
Voice and Style	G	G	G	G	G	C	G	G	G	G
Use of Conventions	G	G	C	C	G	C	G	G	G	O

O = Outstanding; E = Excellent; G = Good; C = Competent (passing); NR = Needs Revision (does not pass the rubric).

Table 7-4 Results of Analysis of Science Research Papers in 1997 Graduation Portfolios

Performance Indicator	Rank								
	44	46	50	56	59	69	71	85
Problem to be Investigated	NR	NR	NR	NR	NR	NR	NR	NR
Experimental/Project Design	C	NR	NR	NR	G	NR	NR	NR
Results	G	NR	NR	NR	C	NR	NR	NR
Analysis of Results	NR	NR	NR	NR	NR	NR	NR	NR

E = Excellent; G = Good; C = Competent (passing); NR = Needs Revision (does not pass the rubric).

Table 7–5 Results of Analysis of Science Research Papers in 1998 Graduation Portfolios

Performance Indicator	Rank										
	34	38	50	56	61	64	68	72	75		
Problem to be Investigated	G	C/NR	C	C	C	C	C	C	C		
Experimental/Project Design	G	C/NR	C	C	C	C	NR	C	C		
Results	G	G	C	C	C	C	NR	NR	C		
Analysis of Results	G	C	C	C	C	C	C	NR	C		

E = Excellent; G = Good; C = Competent (passing); NR = Needs Revision (does not pass the rubric).

Table 7–6 Results of Analysis of Science Research Papers in 1999 Graduation Portfolios

Performance Indicator	Rank											
	49	54	56	57	70	72	77	79	83	85		
Problem to be Investigated	C	C	NR	C/NR	C	NR	C	C	C	C		
Experimental/Project Design	C	C	NR	C/NR	C	NR	C	G	C	G		
Results	C	C	NR	C/NR	C	NR	C	G	C	G		
Analysis of Results	C	C	NR	NR	C	NR	C	C	C	C		

E = Excellent; G = Good; C = Competent (passing); NR = Needs Revision (does not pass the rubric).

on the importance or nature of his contributions or his failings. Another writer has a very clear thesis, "The Vietnam War Was a Mistake," but uses only sources that agree with her thesis. Arguments in defense of this war are not even mentioned. In many respects, this is a strong paper, but the absence of varied perspectives, given the topic, clearly fails to meet the rubric criteria for use of evidence.

In contrast, only three of the eighteen papers from 1998 and 1999 portfolios failed to pass every single rubric criterion. In 1999, five papers matched descriptors for "outstanding" on some of the rubric criteria. One paper made a cogent argument that nationalism was a more important cause of World War I than others posited by historians. Another was a sophisticated analysis of how incursions by the U.S. Government have changed but not destroyed Cheyenne religious practice and belief. The third paper asked the question, "Is the increased temperature of the earth something we need to worry about?" and analyzed both "believers who think that global warming is a huge environmental threat and skeptics who say that global warming doesn't even exist." Two papers endorsed tough gun control laws. Both effectively debunked the common belief that the Second Amendment protects the rights of individuals to bear arms, but one used the Columbine High School shootings and the prevalence of gun accidents to argue for tougher laws while the other relied more on statistical comparisons between countries with strong laws against handguns and the United States. These papers were written for four different teachers in four different courses. They were all written by students who ranked in the bottom half of their class (although not in the bottom quartile). They were written by students from four different language and nationality groups. All this suggests that the promulgation of standards is having a pervasive, broad-reaching effect in our school.

The criterion for which there is still the most room for improvement is the performance indicator called "use of evidence" in the consortium rubric. All eighteen of the 1998 and 1999 papers passed this criterion but ten got the lowest passing score (the "competent" column on the rubric in Figure 7–1). One reason for this underwhelming performance is that while the descriptions under the "competent" columns of the IHS and consortium rubrics are quite similar, the "good" column of the consortium rubric introduces some criteria that are absent from the IHS rubric, including "some evidence drawn from primary sources" and "evaluation of some opposing or varied sources." (The "competent" column describes "adequate use" of primary sources and of opposing/varied sources that I have interpreted as less than some but more than none if the topic really calls for such evidence.) At the time of this study, IHS teachers have been encouraging use of primary sources and analysis of opposing or varied sources, but they were evidently not requiring it. If anything, this supports the underlying thesis of my research—"put it in the rubric and it will be taught," since what is not explicit in the IHS rubric was not as commonly found in our students' papers.

A second reason why IHS students may be weaker in their use of evidence than in other performance indicators is that using evidence is the hardest thing to do well in a research paper. It is one thing to come up with an interesting thesis but quite another to marshal convincing evidence to support it and to effectively counter other explanations or points of view. Student performance can be affected by the limits on time for research and by the limited availability of appropriate sources. Reading varied sources is particularly difficult for English-language learners who must struggle to understand difficult texts written in unfamiliar styles. Experts in language acquisition (Krashen 1981c; Cummins 1981) claim it takes at least seven years to achieve fluency in a second language if one begins to learn it after the onset of adolescence, as is the case with virtually all of our students. Most of our students have been in an English-speaking school system for far less than seven years when they prepare their portfolio projects. Given these constraints, even moderate improvements in our students' performance should be considered noteworthy.

Teacher Interventions

Social studies teachers identify several areas where their practice has changed in response to the portfolio process. One obvious change is in how they grade research papers. One teacher noted that she is harder on juniors and seniors now, thinking about portfolios as she corrects the research papers. One change I have made in my own class is that I first incorporate the research paper rubric in my directions to students, and then ask them to use the actual rubric in giving each other feedback on their first drafts.

Teachers agree they devote more class time to the papers now that the stakes are so high, and they give students more help at every stage. There was general agreement among both social studies and science teachers that the toughest but most important job was helping students understand what a thesis/hypothesis actually is. Everything else grinds to a halt as they guide the students through as many as three drafts. In this process, teachers stress basic skills such as note taking—how to use index cards, how to decide what to take notes on and what is irrelevant, how to take down bibliographic information for future use. Some teachers feel that students have to first write a factual report on a topic before they can formulate a thesis question to investigate.

The teachers' efforts seem to be paying off in terms of increased student awareness. Before introducing a research paper project in my ungraded, multiage class, I asked students to list the five most important things that made a research paper good. Juniors and seniors all listed "thesis" while few sophomores and no freshmen did.

One practice that has clearly changed since the introduction of rubrics is the assigning of research papers as group projects. Several of us were accustomed to asking the students to form groups, explore a topic, and divide up responsibility for completing the work. However, once the rubric was established, some of our students' work was called into question, not because authorship was uncertain, but because not every student's section of a project had a clear thesis. As an example, one teacher

134

used to assign the "Bill of Rights" project as a team effort. In 1997, some of the projects themselves were like portfolios, combining court case summaries, arguments, hypothetical situations, even, in one case, poetry. The overall project generally had a thesis question—for example, Does the First Amendment's guarantee of the right of association apply to gang activity?—but the separate sections did not effectively organize information to resolve the question. This same teacher revised the project as of the 1997–98 school year. Students interested in the same topic—for example, gun control, the death penalty, or school prayer—work at the same table, help each other find sources, and refine and debate the issues. However, each student writes his or her own paper using a tightly prescribed outline. The results, as seen in the 1998 and 1999 portfolios, are some good to outstanding research papers that take a clear position and marshal sources to defend it. The best of the papers deal effectively with opposing or varied points of view.

My own teaching has changed since the rubrics were introduced. I used to assign a group research paper in which students studied immigration from a particular country, each taking a different question: for example, Why did they leave their homes? What attracted them to this country? What was their journey like? What were their lives as new immigrants like? The experience of having to work with others on a sustained, high-stakes project was very useful, with obvious real-life applications. The results, particularly the students' oral presentations, were quite rich. One group did a talk show on the problems of Mexican immigrants. Another imitated an interpreter at the Lower East Side Tenement museum, opening their "home" to the class, staying in character as they answered questions and even serving the class spaghetti! However, when I showed some of the resulting papers to some of my colleagues, they questioned their "portfoliability" because of the lack of explicit thesis questions in most of the sections. Based on this feedback, I changed my strategy. The next year, I started with a group research activity rather than a paper, for example, grouping students so that students at the same table were studying two different immigrant groups that came to this country at similar times. Out of this work, seniors are encouraged to come up with a thesis question for further exploration in a research paper.

Discussion of Science Projects/Experiments

None of the science projects in the baseline year 1997 (pre-rubric) pass all of the rubric performance indicators. Most do not pass any of them. In general, the science projects are even weaker than the social studies research papers. The science papers tend either to be reports listing information with neither thesis nor hypothesis or they are teacher-generated worksheets for classroom activities. For example, one student submitted a paper on how the HIV virus can be contracted. She reports on the conclusions of medical scientists without any evidence of understanding how those conclusions were arrived at. Another student submitted a teacher-made activity that asked students to hypothesize about whether powdered lemonade would dissolve faster in hot or cold water and to explain why. Although the papers may contain worthwhile classroom activities or homework assignments, most are not substantive enough to warrant inclusion in a graduation portfolio regardless of the specifics of the rubric. Little of the 1997 work demonstrates an understanding of the scientific method or applies that understanding to a student-generated project or experiment. To the extent that the rubric descriptions even apply to the 1997 work, it is clearly in the "needs revision" column of the rubric.

In contrast, thirteen of the nineteen projects submitted in 1998 and 1999 scored at least a "competent" on every performance indicator. Although very little of the work can be said to meet the rubric's descriptions of "good," and there were no examples of "outstanding" work, most of the work met the minimum criteria for a science project or experiment—a problem to be investigated, an hypothesis to test, a reasonable design for the experiment or project, adequate observations and data collection, and reporting of results. It's as if there were a wake-up call in the International science labs sometime during the 1997–98

136

school year. Quite possibly that wake-up call came in the fall of 1997 when the newly drafted science rubric was introduced to the staff and prior student portfolio work was seen through the lens of the new rubric. One immediate change was in staffing. New hiring and rearranging of staff assignments ensured that, by the fall of 1998, every student would receive science instruction every year. In any event, the science work produced or revised by seniors for the 1998 and 1999 portfolios is substantially different from work in the prerubric year of 1997.

An example of what changed can be found in a common IHS science project called The Plant Log. This project, actually completed in 1995, appears in a 1997 portfolio. A student planted several seeds and watched them grow, filling in worksheets provided by the teacher. The project is strong on observation. The student recorded a variety of measurements four times per week for a full month and kept a log describing how the plants looked over time. The student also used math to analyze her data. For instance, she produced a series of graphs charting various aspects of the plants' growth over time.

However, despite her diligence, it was unlikely that the student's work would have met the criteria for passing on the consortium rubric because she did not know how to formulate hypotheses. One year later, a student submitted a new version of the Plant Log project, prepared in the spring of 1998. This time, the student wrote that he had been asked to come up with his own hypothesis and to test it with his own experiment. He hypothesized that a plant in perlite (volcanic rock) will germinate and grow faster than plants in regular soil. He included some background research that helped identify his variables. He paid close attention to these variables in his experimental design to make sure that the control plant and the experimental plant grew under identical conditions other than the soil. As did students in previous years, he took frequent measurements and produced sketches, logs, and graphs of growth over time. His analysis of the results was simple but clear: perlite promotes improved aeration and drainage leading to stronger roots, and he proposed new experiments based on his findings. The only obvious flaw was that there were not repeated trials, so that seed characteristics could not be ruled out as the reason why the plant in perlite grew faster and bigger.

Teacher Interventions

It was clear from a comparison of the two versions of the Plant Log project that the teacher had changed it, keeping the instructions on observation, data entry, and the use of math but adding both an experimental component and a requirement for outside research. In other words, a solid classroom activity was transformed into a "portfoliable" project. One of the teachers who assign this project confirmed that she and her colleagues have made a series of changes. For one, she spends more time on giving students practice making scientific predictions and on the various aspects of experimental design. Now, she not only asks students to use math to analyze data but also expects them to actually write in words what the data is telling them. For the Plant Log, she now requires students to read background research about photosynthesis and germination. Students are now instructed to write a hypothesis focusing on changing one variable. Some get their ideas from books while others come up with their own.

There are still a significant number of post-rubric science projects that fail to meet some of the rubric criteria. In at least three instances in the 1999 portfolios, the problem clearly lies with the assigned activity itself: looking at prepared slides through a microscope. The main point of the activity is to teach students how to use a microscope. Although it leads the students through a series of worthwhile observations, it does not call for a hypothesis or experimental design. Thus, no matter how meticulously students do their work, they cannot pass the rubric with this assignment. Interestingly, the teacher who assigns this activity was on sabbatical in 1997–98, the year the IHS science rubric was first introduced. He did not attend a meeting held the following year by the school's science teachers called to discuss what makes a project "portfoliable." As of the 2001–02 school year, a more rigorous version of the project can still be found in some students' portfolios, but the teacher now helps students conduct science experiments as well.

Schoolwide Support

In 1998, International High School was the recipient of a coveted Model Professional Development Award from the U.S. Department of Education. Evaluators were impressed at how, at every level, the school's professional development program is organized around equipping faculty members to support students to meet increasingly rigorous graduation requirements. For example, most faculty meetings during the first four years of portfolio development were devoted to working back from exit criteria to evaluate and improve instruction. Tasks included teams of teachers comparing their projects and activities to the state content standards and revising curricula to ensure that every student has adequate learning opportunities to put together a satisfactory senior portfolio. At other faculty meetings, teachers looked at student work through the lens of the rubrics, not only to come to a common understanding of the rubrics but also to assess what made some student work better than others, how a student could have been guided to improve a particular project, and how teachers could revise assignments to increase the chances they would result in "portfoliable" work. Recently, we have used a faculty meeting to coach each other on how to be an effective mentor (the faculty advisor was assigned to each senior to get them through the process of putting together and presenting a portfolio).

Some of these discussions grouped teachers by the discipline they teach but others were interdisciplinary by design. Thus, for instance, a literature teacher was asked to explain to math, science, and social studies teachers what she meant by a "critical lens." This was very important because teachers serve as senior mentors and must be able to advise students on what constitutes portfoliable work in every subject. Moreover, all teachers serve on the portfolio certification panels that review the portfolios and hear students' presentations. Teachers may tend to ask the defending student questions in their own particular area of expertise, but they must be satisfied that the portfolio as a whole meets rubric requirements.

Another important factor that helps teachers work with students to meet the standards embedded in the rubrics is the school's unique organization. The school currently groups teachers into interdisciplinary teams jointly responsible for the same mixed-age group of students for a full two years. The interdisciplinary instructional teams carry the greatest responsibility and receive the bulk of the resources for doing whatever it takes to help students meet rigorous exit criteria. Team members are aware that come the fall, the school's policymaking body will be looking at the school's graduation data disaggregated by team. If a particular team has a disproportionately low graduation rate, questions will be asked.

Weekly team meetings are built into the school schedule. Team members typically use this collaboration time to revise student assignments to better prepare all students for senior portfolio and to employ a case management approach to adapt those assignments to the needs of specific students. On my team, we have often revised our schedules to support whatever teacher is working with students on a portfolio project. When the big science experiments are under way, we sometimes try to team our science specialist with a second teacher because the student groups need a lot of coaching as they shape their hypotheses and formulate their experimental designs. When it is time for the big research paper, we try to reduce the number of students each humanities teacher sees, so we can give each student lots of feedback on every draft.

Individual teachers mentor individual seniors but rely on the other members of their interdisciplinary team to coach all the teams' seniors in specific subject areas. For example, the science teachers reported that they set up extra class periods to meet with all of their teams' seniors, not just their own mentees, to make sure their science experiments are ready for the graduation portfolio.

The fact that teachers serve as mentors and panel members has made us accountable to each other in new ways. One teacher's pet project becomes everyone's business when the teacher who assigns it holds it out as a portfolio "Performance Based Assessment Task," not just another classroom activity. When we meet with seniors in the fall, we expect them to have some of the portfolio projects either completed or worthy of revising. If they don't, we question not only what they were doing the year before but also what last year's teachers were doing. Similarly, we expect our sophomores and juniors to have had some practice doing literary essays, research papers, science experiments, and applied math, and to be ready for more sophisticated work. We have come to expect that all teachers are providing learning opportunities designed to move our students toward specific proficiencies from the moment they enter our school.

Study Two

In my quest to ascertain the impact of context on student work, I analyzed in detail the writing of three students, comparing responses to one of the test prompts on the ELA Regents with a similar task prepared for class. Two of the students scored above 55, the passing final score for the January 2001 Regents. Only one of these two students scored above 65 (the passing score as of 2003). The third scored 46. Each student is identified by his final test score. Students are discussed in descending test score order.

First, however, it is important to understand how the ELA Regents is scored. There are four essays on this test. For each essay, graders use a rubric that describes six different levels of performance on five criteria—meaning, development, organization, language use, and conventions. Graders then decide what level of performance (1 through 6) best describes the essay as a whole. Two different graders read each essay. If the two scores differ by more than one point the essay is read by yet another grader. There are also multiple-choice questions based on the

Table 7–7 A Comparison of Scores for Five Students on the January 2001 ELA Exam

Final score on January 2001 ELA Regents	Score for Day 2 Part A essay (out of a possible 6)	Total score for 4 essays (out of a possible 24)	Total score for multiple choice (out of a possible 26)
66	3.5	13	21
58	1	9	23
54	3	11	16
52	2.5	11	15
46	3	10	12
42	2	7	15

listening and reading passages that form the basis of three of the essays. The scoring guide comes with a table to convert total essay and multiple-choice scores into a final score. That table changes with each administration of the Regents exam. The same essay scores and multiple-choice scores that result in a given final score on one administration of the test could result in a higher or a lower final score on a different administration. Table 7–7 shows the scores for five students on the January 2001 ELA exam. The student who passed with a 58 had a lower total essay score than some of the students who failed because he did much better than they on the multiple-choice questions.

Student 66

Student 66 was a high-achieving senior whose reading and writing skills were among the best in the school. Her first language is Albanian. She wrote the following during the post-ELA free writing session:

> While taking the Regents, I felt like I was in prison, waiting to die. I was nervous and after a few hours, it was difficult for me to focus and concentrate. I wanted to just get up and leave. But I kept pushing myself to try harder. Now that I got my results, I am truly relieved. I still can't believe I passed both tests. I was pretty sure I failed them both [referring to the ELA and math Regents] . . . The reason why I'm so surprised I passed is because

I know that my work on the tests wasn't anything like my work in class. Luckily, I was able to take my time on the tests. Otherwise, I definitely wouldn't pass. The tests were too long. Especially the English part . . . Boring, difficult, confusing, wouldn't be the perfect words to express my feelings towards the Regents. The tests were!!! *Crazy!!!* In other words, these tests put an enormous amount of pressure on students. Perhaps such pressure we're "supposed" to easily deal with. However, for a student like me, it's difficult.

A comparison of Student 66's response to the ELA prompt and her essay for class (see Table 7–8) demonstrates her seemingly well-founded belief that her work on the test does not accurately reflect the quality of her class work. The feelings she describes above may account for the poorer quality of her work on the test. In any event, her test essay received a score of 3.5 out of a possible 6, placing it in the middle of the rubric. She conveys an understanding of the texts by establishing a central idea but connects this idea to the topic in a cursory way. She develops ideas briefly using some evidence from the texts but the quote she selects does not illustrate her point. She maintains focus but does not address all parts of the controlling idea until the last sentence of her conclusion.

I revisited the grading, using the same rubric, following the format used by the test makers in describing the anchor papers (sample essays provided to illustrate writing at each level to

Table 7–8 Comparison of Student Writing on Two Different Tasks Assessed Using GLA Rubric

Quality	ELA Essay Score	Class Assignment Score
Meaning	4 for idea 3 for connections	5
Development	3	5
Organization	3 or 4	5
Language Use	4	5
Conventions	4 or 5	3 or 4

increase interrater reliability). Based on my analysis, the score Student 66 received was appropriate. Her essay is workmanlike, but rather pedestrian and perfunctory as a response to literature.

In contrast, the same student wrote a passionate essay on two poems of the Harlem Renaissance in response to a classroom assignment. Curiously, she shows less skill with the conventions (possibly because she is taking more risks with what she is trying to express, or possibly because this class assignment was typed, rather than handwritten and reflects less-than-stellar keyboard skills). On the other hand, she makes much more extensive and compelling use of the literary works to develop her central idea than she did in the test response. Looking at this writing sample through the lens of the ELA rubric, it would have received a grade of four or five on the ELA Regents.

Student 58

Student 58 was a hardworking junior whose first language is Arabic. In the fall of 2000, his classroom writing showed that he was having serious problems with organization, verb tenses, pronouns, and syntax (word order). In part, these problems may have reflected the typical tendency of second-language learners to apply L1 (first-language) grammar to L2 (English) writing; they may also have reflected a lack of academic preparation in writing in his home country. In his post-Regents freewrite he observed:

> I felt kind of scare a lttle bit. I feel so happy that I passed, but I don't care about score. Mine was ok "58." The part that I found so hard for me was, the one that was taken on Thursday which is a second part. Like I said I found it so hard for me. The first passage was terrible. So hard to understand.

Here is his entire response to Day Two Part A, the essay he refers to above:

> In this eassy, I am going to talk about both passeges using the idea of discovering of the beauty. Discovering of the beauty is some thing that you have to do to get, you have to work hard,

ask etc. Beauty could be any thing like picture, imagenation to write about so as I was reading my passeges, I learned that even if you want to do something and you do not know about it, at least try, don't give up.

This essay received a score of one. There was minimal evidence of textual understanding and no connections between the texts or among ideas in the texts. There was no evidence of development, no focus or organization. The language is incoherent, and the conventions of English writing are absent.

In June 2001, the same student turned in the Harlem Renaissance poetry assignment (quoted in part below):

> are's self-esteem is greatly affected with how others see us. for example, the little girl in the poem "NO IMAGES" has a negative self-image because of what she was told the standards of beauty were, which is to have white characteristics, and since she didn't fit that criteria she viewed herself as unattractive. ". . . She thinks her brown body has no glory." Also in the poem "IF WE MUST DIE" the black people see their lives as if it was accursed. ". . . Making their (unclear) at our accursed lot." This statement proves the Blacks negative self-images.
>
> To this day some African Americans still suffer from negative self image. As you see, some African Americans females straighten their hair, dying it blonde and wearing blue or green contact lenses. Unconsciously trying to obtain a "white" look. Because the African look has been undermined by centuries of rasicm and negativity towards African American culture. And it most certainly does not apply only for African Americans. People of all races and ages view themselves and turn their self-confidence by what their peers say about them.

This essay would probably receive at least a score of 3 if it were a response on the ELA. Unlike the essay Student 58 wrote for the exam, this classroom assignment does establish a controlling idea and develops ideas briefly, using evidence from the texts. The student "demonstrates emerging control, exhibiting occasional errors that hinder comprehension." His language use demonstrates conviction about his ideas. Like the essay produced by Student 66, Student 58's work had something that the ELA rubric fails to measure or address and that the ELA prompts rarely elicit—passion and engagement.

Student 46

Student 46 is a Spanish-speaking junior whose class work throughout the year indicated that she was a fairly fluent reader but had writing problems regarding organization, language use, and conventions. Generally, her writing was comprehensible enough to demonstrate understanding of texts and to communicate her ideas. She received a score of 3 on the ELA prompt and "Level 3" would probably most accurately describe her response to the classroom assignment as well. Interestingly, in both pieces she was able to effectively interpret passages from the texts but not to create a consistently coherent essay with a clear controlling idea. On the test, she arguably made better use of quotes from the texts than Student 66. For instance, she quotes Annie Dillard describing a swallow that the author saw after an air show, "'that held its wings oddly, tipped them and rolled down the air in loops.' This means all the imagination that she had about the plane. It was a beautiful bird doing all those kind of things in the air." But she does not state the controlling idea related to this quote until the last sentence of the essay, "I think by reading this two passages we should appreciate life for all the beauty that we all have."

Similarly, in her essay for class, she chooses good quotes from the poems and gives them convincing interpretations. For instance, she quotes and interprets the following from "No Images":

'But there are not palm trees on the street, And dishwater gives back no images.' This is where she is living it may be as a slave. The quotes means that when she is washing the plates in the dishwater all the residue of the food don't let her see her beaty. She feels bad about her self. Her selfsteem is low because she cannot see her beauty. She feel like a prisoner because in Africa she could go any where she want."

146

She is less effective at stating her overall point, "if we are treated bad our selfsteem will be low and I will feel bad about word. It is most how the world treat us and people."

The work of these three students suggests that sometimes performance levels will be the same on both on-demand tests and work prepared for class, but it is far from safe to assume that responses to tests are an accurate reflection on how students are able to perform in other contexts on more authentic assignments.

Their freewrites and those of the other students in the class suggest complex reactions to the experience of taking the ELA. All found them a chore and anxiety provoking. Those who failed were distressed that their best was not enough. They also expressed frustration at the results somehow being beyond their control and anger at what they saw as the arbitrary nature of the scoring. Despite the fact that we had reviewed the ELA rubrics with students as part of their preparation for the test, it was clear that they could not incorporate them into the test-taking experience.

Analysis

The introduction of a performance-based assessment system, with clear guidelines for assessing student projects and substantial time devoted to professional development has led to changes in teacher practice that have led to improved student performance. What is alternative about this system is not the standards themselves but how mastery of these standards is assessed. Teachers understand how to teach to these standards because it has been a matter of constant discussion in the school. Teaching to standards does not mean prepping students for unfamiliar tests. Rather, it means, as Wiggins and McTighe (2001) describe, helping students complete substantive projects. This seems to be what made the portfolio assessments meaningful to the students and what was lacking with respect to the ELA test.

There is a wide body of research around this type of performance-based assessment. One argument in the research suggests that performance-based assessment eliminates the "black box" effect of external tests with tight test security. While students do better if they know very concretely what standards they will be held to and are given assignments that allow them to develop mastery and then to demonstrate it, the context, as my research demonstrates, is key. Unlike the detailed responses that teachers give students to classroom assignments, students get only one piece of information about their performance on the Regents—a passing or failing score. When they work on a portfolio project, they have the opportunity to review their early drafts of the project against the portfolio rubric for the project. They discuss with teachers what next steps to take to make their ideas clearer or to more effectively marshal evidence to support those ideas. Students are in the driver's seat. They not only have the criteria in front of them while they are working; they also have every opportunity to keep working to meet those criteria. Naturally, we reviewed the ELA rubrics with students as part of their preparation for the test, but on the day of the test, they did not and could not have those rubrics in front of them. And they had no chance to revise their work after comparing it to the rubrics. The point of assessment is not just to monitor performance but also to improve it (Wiggins 1993, 200).

Another argument about performance-based assessment is that it is a better assessment to "teach to" than one on-demand test. As Grant Wiggins observes, defenders of traditional testing fail to see that "it is the form, not the content of the test that is harmful to learning" (1990, 2). No test, no matter how good it is, can demonstrate the reflection, revision, and sustained effort over time contained in substantial portfolio projects like those that are under way at IHS. If high-stakes decisions are made based on one-shot tests, both teachers and students "are led to believe that right answers matter more than habits of mind and the justification of one's approach and results" (Wiggins 1990, 2). If the intended outcome of teaching is to equip students for their roles as citizens, then "we must give less emphasis to mere recall and low-level comprehension of facts and concepts and more emphasis to applying knowledge to tasks that require high-level cognition" (Nickell 1997, 3).

A third argument for performance-based assessment is that it assesses what is most important rather than simply what is convenient to test. In writing about the many forms that human intelligence takes, Mindy Kornhaber and her colleagues warn "unless assessment is placed in the context of authentic domains and social environments, we doubt it can adequately represent human intellectual performance." In other words, they warn against tests that "require people to deal with atypical, decontextualized tasks, rather than probing how people function when they are able to draw upon their experience, feedback, and knowledge as they typically do" (Kornhaber, Krechevsky, and Gardner 1990, 188–89). The contrast between the performance of Student 66 on the ELA and on the class writing assignment demonstrates this well.

Although the structures of the two tasks—the test response and the classroom assignment—were virtually identical, the experience for students was quite different. For one, the Regents essay must be completed in one sitting. (Because our students are English Language Learners, they receive more time to write the essay, but they still must complete it before they leave the building on the day of the test.) In contrast, students have about a week to complete the homework assignment. They have time to let their ideas percolate and to revise their writing as much as they like before I first see it. Second, the content of reading material on the Regents is not grounded in anything the students have been studying or in their personal experiences. Third, the Regents essay is written under pressure, and students must deal with the typical on-demand testing jitters. These jitters are amplified by the simple fact that until they pass the ELA Regents, they will not receive a high school diploma.

So far, no student has failed to graduate our school solely because of the ELA Regents even though we are a school of English Language Learners. Our success is due, in part, to the emphasis we have always placed on developing English skills. The portfolio projects themselves play an important role in developing advanced reading and writing skills. Moreover, we have seniors who have passed the ELA but are not ready to present their portfolios, either because they need more English before they are ready to master research papers and science experiments or because they have not mastered the art of sustaining effort over time.

Our students' success on the ELA is also a reflection of how the state's instructions for scoring make the ELA a relatively easy test to pass, mainly because a high score on the multiple-choice reading comprehension questions can make up for very poor scores on the essays. We have had several students who were in an earlier cohort that was required to pass only the Regents Competency Test. They tried and failed several times to pass the RCT in reading but were able to pass the seemingly more difficult ELA. All this may change when the passing score on the ELA Regents goes up to 65. On the other hand, the state could easily manipulate the tables used for determining the final score to prevent too many students from failing while at the same time appearing to raise the performance bar.

Although we have seen gradual improvement over time in response to our more rigorous portfolio process, we are concerned about how our students will do on the two history Regents and on the science Regents. A 1997 study of English Language Learners found that "Students of all ages reached grade-level achievement in mathematics and language arts . . . in a shorter period of time, but required many years to reach grade level in reading, science and social studies in English" Thomas and Collier (1997, 36) write that students who arrive after age twelve, even with good formal schooling in their native language, "had (by the end of high school) run out of time to catch up academically to the native English speakers, who were continually pulling ahead." However, the author notes, "Students with limited literacy in native language will take even longer to learn the English skills associated with science, social studies and higher order mathematics" (Thomas and Collier 1997, 36).

Conclusion and Policy Implications

The comparison of student writing on a high-stakes test and their work on a classroom assignment highlights the dual dangers of allowing one on-demand test to define a student's readiness to graduate. As this study demonstrates, for many students, an on-demand test is not the best way to demonstrate mastery of skills and knowledge. Multiple forms of assessment offer a fuller, fairer picture of achievement. As Orfield and Wald note in an article on high-stakes testing, "National testing experts, the National Research Council, the American Educational Research Association, the American Psychological Association, the National Council on Measurement in Education and the Department of Education all assert that no decision of serious consequence in a child's life should be made on the basis of a single test score" (Orfield and Wald 2001, 2).

While a high-stakes test will not prevent many students from graduating, focusing too much on the narrow set of skills required to pass the test fails to provide students with in-depth, challenging performance tasks. As the American Evaluation Association observed in its position statement on high-stakes testing in preK-12 education, "the simplistic application of single tests or test batteries to make high stakes decisions about individuals and groups impede rather than improve student learning." Among the problems associated with high stakes testing is that it can "draw schools into narrow conceptions of teaching and education that leave children deprived of the history, cultural perspective, personal experience and interdisciplinary nature of subject matter" (American Evaluation Association 2002, 1–2).

The very testing schemes that were intended to hold schools accountable for serving disadvantaged subgroups tend to adversely affect those groups. This happens when groups less likely to score well are held back or pushed out or when well-intentioned educators narrow the curriculum and focus on test preparation over meaningful mastery of content or skills. It also happens when the tests are not the most effective way of demonstrating mastery and yet can prevent a student from getting a high school diploma. English Language Learners are the canaries in the assessment mine. The lack of native proficiency in English makes them particularly vulnerable to the inherent problems of on-demand testing, including arbitrary and unrealistic time limits, lack of context or meaning in the assessment tasks, inappropriate assumptions about prior knowledge, and unfamiliarity with vocabulary and idiom.

An effective portfolio assessment elicits and evaluates competencies beyond the scope of standardized tests. Even the best of such tests cannot measure the skills of posing good questions, going beyond the surface to find answers, maintaining a sustained effort over time, and taking time for reflection and revision. Nor do they address state standards for oral communication—a central part of the portfolio presentations that students make before a panel of teachers, peers, and outside guests. On-demand tests are at best proxies for the real work that students, workers, and citizens must do. For instance, the Regents prompt simulates the experience of reading works of literature to formulate and discuss important ideas. The Harlem Renaissance classroom assignment *is* that experience.

It appears virtually certain, barring a victory in the courts, that International will have to give five high-stakes tests, any one of which can prevent an otherwise qualified student from graduating. It is highly unlikely that the graduation portfolio assessment system can be maintained in its present state, let alone shared with additional schools. In most schools it would be impossible to prepare students simultaneously for two very different assessment systems. Even assuming teachers and students are willing to put in the hard work necessary for portfolio assessment that "doesn't count" toward meeting state graduation requirements, the first consideration would have to be to adequately prepare students for whatever does count.

Schools that are willing and able to institute performance assessments that not only incorporate state standards but also help students achieve them deserve the encouragement and support of their districts and states. To sustain and expand performance assessment systems such as those in place at International and the other consortium schools, specific kinds of support must be in place at the school, district, and state level. The experience at International High School shows that to be an engine for improved student performance, the assessment system must be created, tested, revised, and constantly revisited by the teachers themselves, not some distant third party. This requires:

- close attention to national, state, and local content and performance standards
- faculty time to decide what projects to include in high-stakes assessment judging criteria
- several years to align curriculum to relevant standards and to prepare students to meet those standards through execution of portfolio projects
- ample faculty time set aside over the course of implementation for:
  - evaluating teacher assignments and student responses to those assignments in light of the criteria students must meet to pass high-stakes assessment
  - coaching teachers on how to better meet the needs of diverse learners attempting to complete these demanding assignments
  - one-on-one mentoring of students to help them meet the standards
- freedom from other assessments that require other kinds of staff development and class activities, including practice for timed tests that by their very nature require specific test-taking skills.

As the public relies more and more on test scores to hold schools accountable, it becomes increasingly important that the assessment systems themselves be held accountable. When tests are used to determine who is promoted and who receives a high school diploma, everything about the testing instruments themselves and related school policies and practices must be carefully scrutinized.

Postscript

In his April 2000 decision letter, the New York State Education Commissioner denied the New York Assessment Consortium's application for a variance from the Regents testing program because the portfolio assessments did not meet his criteria for validity, reliability, and connection to the state's academic standards for students. He defined those criteria narrowly as they apply to on-demand testing. The irony here is that his own testing program violates a central tenet of assessment that no one instrumentality be used to make high-stakes decisions such as who may graduate. Because the portfolio system did not look like on-demand testing, the commissioner rejected it when he might well have seen it as a useful way to overcome the fatal flaw of the Regents testing system—the lack of multiple forms of evidence to evaluate student mastery.

The commissioner did not forbid portfolio assessments; rather, he denied their value in determining who graduates. He wrote:

> This decision does not say that the schools must stop using portfolios, projects and culminating presentations. Those assessments appear to resemble a series of locally developed assessments. All schools have local assessments to some extent, and some use elements similar to what Consortium schools use. The distinction here is between local assessments used for adjudging course completion and the assessments that can be approved for State purposes of measuring achievement of the State Learning Standards. For the latter purposes, only Regents examinations or approved alternatives can be used (The State Education Department of the State of New York 2000).

The commissioner's decision brushes away with a few pen strokes many years of effort on the part of teachers participating in a large and influential grassroots movement to improve both teaching and assessment. This ignores an important tenet in school reform eloquently laid out in *The Teaching Gap*:

> Teachers must be at the heart of the solution. Not only are they the gatekeepers for all improvement efforts, they are also in the best position to acquire the knowledge that is needed. They are, after all, the only ones who can improve teaching. Proposals that do not recognize this truth cannot succeed (Stigler and Hiebert 1999, 174).

8

Bringing the Voice of Teachers into Education Policy

Ellen Meyers and Frances O'Connell Rust

From its beginning in 1979, Teachers Network has sought to provide a forum for teachers to share their insights and practice. However, in 1989 a noticeable absence of the teachers' voice in education policy reform sparked the initiative now called the Teachers Network Policy Institute. That was the year of the first National Education Summit called by President George H. W. Bush and led by then governor Bill Clinton. Not one teacher was invited. That same year, to commemorate its tenth anniversary, Teachers Network asked City College of New York architecture students to design a school of the future. The architecture students, in turn, solicited the input of teachers from IMPACT II (Teachers Network's flagship program), asking them to dream of the ideal school. Their answers were surprisingly basic—"more outlets," "clean hallways," and "unbroken windows."

The task was clear: Teachers had to become engaged in thinking beyond the dailiness of schools. They had to enter the discourse of education policy. It was recognized that no matter how well intentioned, policies coming out of summits and statehouses, far removed from classrooms, could not be successfully implemented if teachers were not part of the process that informs policy creation. To be invited to summits and statehouses, teachers had to become articulate about their positions on critical issues in the education policy debate. However, without the evidence that comes from systematic examination and assessment of practice, the teachers' voice would be neither focused nor heeded. Education policy would remain incomplete, its implementation compromised.

Getting Started

To heed the call, Teachers Network launched the New York City Teacher Policy Institute in 1995. In the following year, Teachers Network expanded the initiative nationwide to create a broader and deeper teacher-based policy group—the Teachers Network Policy Institute (TNPI). TNPI began as a group of thirty-five elementary, middle, and high school teachers. These teachers, all of whom maintain full-time classroom responsibilities, were chosen to become TNPI MetLife Fellows because of their reputations for leadership and work toward demonstrable change within their schools. TNPI now numbers one hundred and fifty teacher-fellows from ten Teachers Network affiliates— Los Angeles; Santa Barbara County, CA; Santa Clara County, CA; Chicago; New York City; Fairfax County, VA; Miami; Charlotte, NC; Lexington, KY; and the State of Wyoming. From the beginning, TNPI's mission has been to give teachers an active voice in education policymaking so that education mandates are informed by the realities of daily classroom life and are aimed at improving the condition of our nation's schools and producing real results in student learning.

In its first two years, TNPI Fellows produced two books: *If We Want to Give Our Children the Best Possible Education, Then . . .* (Teachers Network 1996), a book that investigates the role of public school teachers in education policymaking. This book evolved from a series of discussions among New York City teachers. The second book, *Getting Real and Getting Smart* (Teachers Network 1998) grew out of reviews of research the fellows had done that focused on teacher preparation and new-teacher induction, ongoing teacher professional growth, teacher networks, and teacher leadership in school change.

In 1998, TNPI Fellows nationwide committed themselves to action research studies in their classrooms and schools. From this work have come three volumes, *TNPI—A Guidebook for Connecting Policy to Practice for Improving Schools* (Teachers Network 2000a), offering a blueprint for teacher groups and other education organizations interested in developing a TNPI affiliate; *What Matters Most—Improving Student Achievement* (Teachers Network 2000b), connecting the findings of the teachers' action research studies with the recommendations of the National Commission on Teaching and America's Future (NCTAF); and *Ensuring Teacher Quality* (Teachers Network 2002), buttressing four recommendations to school district superintendents on how to attract and retain quality teachers.

From Action Research to School Reform

This book is the first collection of action research by TNPI Fellows. Our intent is to demonstrate how teachers in the course of their everyday teaching can make the case for school reform. While action research has been a valuable method for the educational community to help teachers understand and reshape their practice, we now know that inquiry-oriented teachers can use action research to communicate to a larger audience how policy affects student learning. These studies show how, as a group of teachers, the TNPI Fellows have begun to draw on their research to influence policy in the following domains: resources needed to meet standards, conditions of the workplace, and the status of the teaching profession.

Making the Case

In his efforts to help all of his students meet the state language arts standards, Matt Wayne struggled with a lack of appropriate resources. His study makes the case for teachers having purchasing power with regard to classroom materials, and decision-making authority with regard to their own professional development. He advocates that teachers conduct action research in their classrooms and convene routinely to share their research, reflect on their practice, and develop action plans for instructional improvement.

Through extensive documentation of the interactions among a group of teachers participating in a professional development network, Jane Fung makes the case for supporting teacher networks as an important strategy for improving teaching practice and supporting new teachers. To implement this strategy, she recommends providing opportunities during the school day for veteran and new teachers to collaborate regularly and incentives to bring more teachers into such networks.

Lara Goldstone's study exposes the challenges of meeting standards in multicultural classrooms. In order for her non-English-speaking students to successfully reach the English Language Arts standards, Goldstone had to involve their families and instigate change at the school, district, and union levels. She extended the time for parent conferences, monopolized the district translator, and called attention to the fact that the standards had not been translated into the language of her students and their families. As a result of her well-documented inquiry, Goldstone's school and district changed their rules and procedures for parent conferences and home–school communications.

The two major issues examined in Carol Tureski's study—time and choice—are fundamental to all teachers' work. Her research on second-language learners demonstrates how powerful it can be for students to choose high-interest books and have ample time to dig into them. To reform the current system that militates against this type of teaching and learning, Tureski makes the case for teachers to have a primary role in school scheduling and to be able to purchase books directly from distributors.

Janet Price takes on the highly politicized issue of assessment and exposes the limitations of high-stakes testing for assessing student learning and reveals its impact on curriculum and instruction. Price makes the case for multiple forms of assessment that are created, tested, revised, and constantly revisited by teachers. She also demonstrates that when faculty work together to assess learning, the school culture shifts to a focus on the quality of instruction and, ultimately, the standard of practice throughout the school improves.

Natasha Warikoo's study provides clear evidence that class size makes a difference in student learning and can have a profound impact on teaching. She also makes the case that the maximum benefits from reduced class size are realized when accompanied by relevant and ongoing professional development that includes peer mentoring based on classroom observations.

Taken together, these studies offer solutions to what many characterize as intractable problems standing in the way of school reform. They spell out what resources are needed and make it clear that these must include time for teachers to work together; high-interest, culturally relevant materials; and professional development that is specifically designed to meet the needs of teachers. They offer concrete suggestions for how to change the conditions of the workplace. These include reducing class size; creating schedules to allow for collaboration, mentoring, and observation; and establishing networks among teachers. These studies illuminate what it will take to raise the status of teaching: decision-making authority about critical issues such as scheduling, purchasing, professional development, and assessment.

We believe that our best hope for school reform will come from the hard work of teachers like these TNPI Fellows. It is through sharing true stories of practice, supported by data, that teachers' voices will become part of the policy discussion. It is incumbent upon the education community to make the link between policy and what actually happens in classrooms. This is a start. When all of us raise our voices together, then we will create real school reform.

References

Allen, J. 1995. *It's Never Too Late: Leading Adolescents to Life-long Literacy*. Portsmouth, NH: Heinemann.

American Association of University Women. 1992. *How Schools Shortchange Girls*. Washington, DC: National Education Association.

American Evaluation Association. 2002. Position Statement on High Stakes Testing in PreK–12 Education. Available online at www.wval.org.

Argys, L., D. Rees, and D. Brewer. 1996. "Detracking America's Schools: Equity at Zero Cost?" *Journal of Policy Analysis and Management* 15: 623–45.

Arnold, P. 2002. "Cooperating Teachers' Professional Growth through Supervision of Student Teachers and Participation in a Collegial Study Group." *Teacher Education Quarterly*, 29(2): 123–132.

Ascher, C. 1983. "Improving the Mathematical Skills of Low Achievers." New York: *ERIC/CUE Fact Sheet* 18.

Atwell, N. 1998. *In the Middle: New Understandings About Writing, Reading, and Learning*. Portsmouth, NH: Boynton/Cook.

Calhoun, E. F. 1994. *How to Use Action Research in the Self-Renewing School*. Alexandria, Va: Association for Supervision and Curriculum Development.

Cizek, G. 1999. "How Cartoons and Calculators Resolved the Class-Size Debate." *Education Week* (December 8).

———. 2000. "Class-Size Essayist Responds to Critics." *Education Week* (January 19): 43.

Cochran-Smith, M., and S. Lytle. 1993. *Inside/Outsider: Teacher Research and Knowledge*. New York: Teachers College Press.

Comer, J. 1988. *Waiting for a Miracle: Why Schools Can't Solve Our Problems—And How We Can*. New York: NAL/Dutton.

Cummins, J. 1981. "The Role of Primary Language Development in Promoting Educational Success for Language Minority Students." In *Schooling and Language Minority Students: A Theoretical Framework*, California State Department of Education, 3–49. Los Angeles: Evaluation, Dissemination, and Assessment Center at California State University, Los Angeles.

Cunningham, A. E., and K. E. Stanovich. 1998. "What Reading Does for the Mind." *American Educator* 22 (Spring): 8.

Cunningham, P., and R. Allington. 1999. *Classrooms That Work: They Can All Read and Write.* 2d ed. Boston, MA: Addison-Wesley.

Darling-Hammond, L. 1997a. *The Right to Learn: A Blueprint for Creating Schools that Work.* San Francisco: Jossey-Bass.

———. 1997b. "What Matters Most: 21st Century Teaching." *Educational Digest* 63 (November): 4–9.

———. 1998. "Teachers and Teaching: Testing Policy Hypotheses from a National Commission Report." *Educational Researcher* 27 (January–February): 5–15.

Elkind, D. 1970. *Children and Adolescents: Interpretive Essays on Jean Piaget.* New York: Oxford University Press.

Ellis, T. 1984. *Class Size.* Eugene, OR: ERIC Clearinghouse on Educational Management.

Epstein, J. 1987. "Parent Involvement: What Research Says to Administrators." *Education and Urban Society* 19 (2): 119–36.

———. 1988. *Homework Practices, Achievements, and Behaviors of Elementary School Students.* Baltimore, MD: Center for Research on Elementary and Middle Schools, Johns Hopkins University.

Fillmore, L. W. 1990. "Now or Later? Issues Related to the Early Education of Minority Group Children." In *Early Childhood and Family Education: Analysis and Recommendations of the Council of Chief State School Officers*, Council of Chief State School Officers, 122–44. Orlando, FL: Harcourt Brace Jovanovich.

Finn, C., and M. Petrilli. 1998. "The Elixir of Class Size." *The Weekly Standard* (March 9).

Finn, J. D. 1998. *Class Size and Students at Risk: What Is Known? What Is Next?* Washington, DC: National Institute on the Education of At-Risk Students.

Fuller, W. 2001. Action Research Study. Unpublished study from the Teachers Network Policy Institute, New York.

Garcia, G. 2000. *Lessons from Research: What Is the Length of Time It Takes Limited English Proficient Students to Acquire English and Succeed in an All-English Classroom?* Issue Brief. Washington, DC: National Clearinghouse for Bilingual Education.

Glass, G., and M. L. Smith. 1978. *Meta-Analysis of Research on the Relationship of Class-Size and Achievement.* San Francisco: Far West Laboratory for Educational Research and Development.

Grabe, W. 1991. "Current Developments in Second Language Reading Research." *TESOL Quarterly* 25 (3): 375–406.

Grashow, M. 2001. "Who Knows Our Children? The Role of Peer Support Groups in the Social and Academic Development of Our Children." Unpublished study from the Teachers Network Policy Institute, New York.

Henderson, A. T., and N. Berla, eds. 1994. *A New Generation of Evidence: The Family is Critical to Student Achievement.* Washington DC: National Commission for Citizens in Education.

Hoxby, C. 2000. "The Effects of Class Size on Student Achievement: New Evidence from Population Variation." *Quarterly Journal of Economics* 115: 1239–85.

Hubbard, R. S., and B. M. Power. 1993. *The Art of Classroom Inquiry: A Handbook for Teacher-Researchers.* Portsmouth, NH: Heinemann.

Institute for Learning. 1998a. *Accountable Talk and Classroom Discussion.* Pittsburgh: Learning Research and Development Center.

————. 1998b. *Indicators of Accountable Talk.* Pittsburgh: Learning Research and Development Center.

————. 1998c. *Looking for Signs of Accountable Talk in a School.* Pittsburgh: Learning Research and Development Center.

Ivey, G. 2000. Redesigning Reading Instruction. *Educational Leadership* 58 (1): 42–45.

Johnson, J., and Duffett, A. 1999. *Standards and Accountability. Where the Public Stands.* New York: Public Agenda.

Kellaghan, T., K. Sloane, B. Alvarez, and B. Bloom. 1993. *The Home Environment and School Learning: Promoting Parental Involvement in the Education of Children.* San Francisco: Jossey-Bass.

Kihn, P. 2001. "Physical Environment and Student Engagement." Unpublished study from the Teachers Network Policy Institute. New York.

Kornhaber, M., M. Krechevsky, and H. Gardner. 1990. "Engaging Intelligence." *Educational Psychologist* 53 (3–4): 177–99.

Krashen, S., ed. 1981a. *Child-Adult Differences in Second Language Attainment.* Rowley, MA: Newbury House.

————. 1981b. "Bilingual Education and Second Language Acquisition Theory." In *Schooling and Language Minority Students: A Theoretical Framework,* California State Department of Education, 51–70. Los Angeles: Evaluation, Dissemination, and Assessment Center at California State University.

————. 1981c. *Second Language Acquisition and Second Language Learning.* London: Pergamon Press.

Krueger, A. 1999. Experimental Estimates of Educational Production Functions. *Quarterly Journal of Economics* 114 (2): 305–42.

Krulik, N. 1997. *Doug's Vampire Caper.* New York, Disney Press.

Lampert, M. 1986. "Knowing, Doing, and Teaching Multiplication." *Cognition and Instruction* 3: 305–42.

Molnar, A., P. Smith, and J. Zahorik. 1999. *Executive Summary: 1998–99 Results of the Student Achievement Guarantee in Edu-*

cation (SAGE) Program Evaluation. Milwaukee: University of Wisconsin-Milwaukee.

Mullin, C., and J. Swanitz. 1999. "Action Research Study." Unpublished study from the Teachers Network Policy Institute, New York.

Murane, R., and F. Levy. 1997. *The New Basic Skills*. New York: Free Press.

National Commission on Excellence in Education. 1983. *A Nation at Risk: The Imperative for Educational Reform*. Washington DC: National Commission on Excellence in Education. Available online at www.ed.gov/pubs/NatAtRisk/index.html.

New York City Board of Education. 1997. *New Standards Performance Standards*. New York: NYCBOE. Available online at www.nycenet.edu/dis/standards/applied.

Nickell, P. 1997. *Alternative Assessment: Implications of Social Studies*. Syracuse, NY: ERIC Digest.

Orfield, G., and J. Wald. 2001. "High Stakes Testing." *In Motion Magazine* (29 April). Available online at www.inmotionmagazine.com/er/gojw.html.

Peregoy, S., and O. Boyle. 1997. *Reading, Writing, and Learning in ESL: A Resource Book for K–12 Teachers*. New York: Longman.

Peterson, L. 2001. "If I Could Put Time in a Bottle: A Study of Teacher Time Use Outside the Classroom." Unpublished study from the Teachers Network Policy Institute, New York.

Picard, S. 2001. "Teacher Talk: Collaborative Conversations About Second Grade Readers." Unpublished study from the Teachers Network Policy Institute, New York.

Pritchard, I. 1999. *Reducing Class Size: What Do We Know?* Washington DC: National Institute on Student Achievement, Curriculum and Assessment.

Resnick, L. 1987. *Education and Learning to Think*. Washington DC: National Academy Press.

———. 1988. "Mathematics as an Ill-Structured Discipline." In *The Teaching and Assessing of Mathematical Problem Solving,* ed. R. Charles, E. Sliver, 32–60. Hillsdale, NJ: Lawrence Erlbaum Associates.

Resnick, L., and D. Resnick. 1989. "Tests as Standards of Achievement in Schools." Princeton, NJ: Educational Testing Service.

Rosenblatt, L. 1978. *The Reader, the Text, the Poem: The Transactional Theory of the Literacy Work.* Carbondale: Southern Illinois Press.

Shields, P., J. Marsh, and J. Powell. 1998. *An Inventory of the Status of Teacher Development in California.* Menlo Park, CA: SRI International.

Slavin, R. 1990. "Achievement Effects of Ability Grouping in Secondary Schools: A Best Evidence Synthesis." *Review of Educational Research* 60: 471-99.

Snyder, L. 1999. "New Teachers: Making Sense from Theory." *Instructional Quarterly* 2 (Spring): 6–7.

Stigler, J. W., and J. Hiebert. 1999. *The Teaching Gap.* New York: Free Press.

Takenaga-Taga, D. 2001. "An Analysis of Preservice Teachers' Views of Five Scientists at Work." Unpublished study from the Teachers Network Policy Institute, New York.

Teachers Network. 1996. *If We Want to Give Our Children the Best Possible Education, Then . . .* New York: Teachers Network.

———. 1998. *Getting Real and Getting Smart.* New York: Teachers Network.

———. 2000a. *TNPI—A Guidebook for Connecting Policy to Practice for Improving Schools.* New York: Teachers Network.

———. 2000b. *What Matters Most: Improving Student Achievement.* New York: Teachers Network.

———. 2002. *Ensuring Teacher Quality: A Report from the MetLife Fellows in the Teachers Network Policy Institute.* New York: Teachers Network.

The State Education Department of the State of New York. 2000. *Decision of the Commissioner: The New York Performance*

Standards Consortium Request for an Extension of a Variance to Use Certain Assessments in Place of the Regents Exams. Albany: State Education Department of the State of New York.

Thomas, D. 1957. "A Refusal to Mourn the Death by Fire of a Child in London." *Collected Poems of Dylan Thomas*. New York: New Directions.

Thomas, W., and V. Collier. 1997. *School Effectiveness for Language Minority Students*. NCBE Resource Collection, no. 9. Washington, DC: National Clearinghouse for Bilingual Education.

Tureski, C. 2000. "Community Building: It's More Than Just Breaking the Ice." Unpublished study from the Teachers Network Policy Institute, New York.

Wayne, M. 2000. "Getting Smarter at School: A 7th Grade Class Researches and Reflects on Its Discussion Habits." Unpublished study from the Teachers Network Policy Institute, New York.

Wenglinsky, H. 1997. *When Money Matters: How Educational Expenditures Improve Student Performance and How They Don't*. Princeton, NJ: The Educational Testing Service, Policy Information Center.

Wiggins, G. 1990. *The Case for Authentic Assessment*. Washington, DC: U.S. Dept. of Education, Office of Educational Research and Improvement, Educational Resources Information Center.

———. 1993. "Assessment Authenticity, Context, and Validity." *Phi Delta Kappan* 75 (3): 200–08, 210–14.

Wiggins, G., and J. McTighe. 2001. *Understanding by Design*. Upper Saddle River, NJ: Merrill/Prentice Hall.

Word, E., C. M. Achilles, H. Bain, J. Folger, J. Johnston, and N. Lintz. 1990. *Project STAR Final Executive Summary Report*. Nashville: Tennessee State Department of Education.

Zeni, J. 2001. *Ethical Issues in Practitioner Research*. New York: Teachers College Press.

About the Contributors

Jane Ching Fung is a public school teacher in Los Angeles, California. She is in her fifteenth year of teaching and learning. Her teaching experience includes primary grades K–3, multiage (PreK–2), Reading Recovery, District Intern Program, and facilitating professional development at the school and district level. Along with her work in mentoring preservice and in-service teachers, Jane helped create The Early Literacy Club in 1994, a new teacher network that continues today.

Jane is a MetLife Fellow in the Teachers Network Policy Institute. She is an active member of the Center for the Future of Teaching and Learning's California Teacher Leadership Forum. She is National Board Certified as an Early Childhood Generalist and holds a master's degree in teaching reading and language arts. A past recipient of the Rotary Club's Outstanding Teacher Award and the Excellence in Education Award, Jane's professional interests include: early literacy, new-teacher support and retention in inner-city schools, teacher networks, and quality professional development.

Lara Goldstone teaches seventh-grade humanities and reading at Camino Nuevo Charter Academy, a small, public middle school near downtown Los Angeles. After having spent almost one-third of her life with young teens in a classroom, Lara is looking forward to devoting part of each day in 2002–2003 to coaching new teachers and facilitating professional development networks at her school. She is also currently on the faculty at California State University, Dominguez Hills, where she instructs new teachers in literacy methodologies.

Over the past nine years, Lara has taught middle school in Oakland, California, and in Manhattan's Chinatown. She has been the recipient of a Chase Active Learning Grant, a Disney grant, and an IMPACT II award for various interdisciplinary curriculum projects she developed with her colleagues. She is passionate about the necessity of opportunity-to-learn standards for all students, the power of teacher collaboration around student work, and the need for inner-city schools to engage parents meaningfully in their childrens' learning.

Ellen Meyers is a founder and senior vice president of Teachers Network, and director of the Teachers Network Policy Institute. She also serves as editor-in-chief of the *By Teachers, For Teachers* series of handbooks; and director of new affiliate development. Additional responsibilities include public relations, fundraising, presentations, and program development.

Ellen has developed the Teachers' Voice Initiative, a program to empower teachers to create school change (1989–present); Teachers Network Policy Institute (1995–present); Global TeachNet, a collaboration with the National Peace Corps Association (1995–98); and the *National Teachers Summit* (1993). She is editor-in-chief of Teachers Network's publications, including *How to Use the Internet in the Classroom* (2001); *New Teachers Handbook* (1998); and *Teachers Guide to Cyberspace* (1996) with disk. She is also the editor, with Frances Rust, of *Ensuring Teacher Quality* (2002), *What Matters Most: Improving Student Achievement* (2000), and *TNPI: A Guidebook for Connecting Policy to Practice for Improving Schools* (2000). Ellen produced the film *Where Have All the Teachers Gone?* aired on PBS, and the videotapes *Inventing the Future of Teaching, The Teachers Network,* and *The Teachers Vision.* She also authored *Changing Schools, Changing Roles—Redefining the Role of the Principal in a Restructured School* and produced the companion videotape, *In It Together—Building Teacher-Principal Collaboration* (1995).

Ellen served as advisory board member of the Wallace–Reader's Digest Funds on Educational Leadership and as consultant to the U.S. Department of Education for the Technology Challenge Program (1996) and the Fund for the Improvement and Reform of Schools (1994). She is currently teaching undergraduates at New York University's Steinhardt School of Education, Department of Teaching and Learning.

Janet Ruth Price teaches humanities at International High School at LaGuardia Community College, a public high school serving new immigrants. Janet has served as a MetLife Fellow in the Teachers Network Policy Institute and as a member of the Education Commission of the States' Governors' Advisory Council on Teacher Quality. She chairs her school's Curriculum and Assessment Committee. Her work with English Language Learners has been documented on video by the Stanford University School of Education.

Before entering the teaching profession, Janet served as executive vice president of New Visions for Public Schools and managing attorney for Advocates for Children of New York, Inc. She has chaired the Committee on Education and the Law of the Association of the Bar of the City of New York and spent a year in residence at Columbia University as a Revson Fellow for the Future of the City of New York. Janet is a co-author of "Student Empowerment Through the Professional Development of Teachers," in the textbook *Paradigm Debates in Curriculum and Supervision* (Bergin and Garvey 2000); *The Multiple Forms of Evidence Study: Assessing Reading Through Student Work Samples, Teacher Observations, and Tests* (New Visions for Public Schools reprinted by NCREST 1994); and the ACLU *Rights of Students* (Southern Illinois University 1989).

Frances O'Connell Rust serves as the university advisor to the Teachers Network Policy Institute. She is professor and coordinator of Early Childhood and Elementary Curricula in the Department of Teaching and Learning, Steinhardt School of Education, New York University. She is the recipient of the 2001 Association of Teacher Educators Award for Distinguished Research in Teacher Education, the Teachers College, Columbia University Outstanding Alumni Award (1998), and the 1985 AERA Outstanding Dissertation Award.

Frances' books include *Guiding School Change: New Understandings of the Role and Work of Change Agents*, which she edited with Helen Freidus (Teachers College Press 2001) and *Changing Teaching, Changing Schools: Bringing Early Childhood*

171

Practice into Public Education (Teachers College Press 1993). For the Teachers Network Policy Institute, Frances has worked with Ellen Meyers to edit *Ensuring Teacher Quality* (2002), *What Matters Most: Improving Student Achievement* (2000), and *TNPI: A Guidebook for Connecting Policy to Practice for Improving Schools* (2000). Recent articles on teaching and teacher education have appeared in the *Journal of Early Childhood Teacher Education, Social Science Record,* the *Journal of Teacher Education,* and *Teaching and Teacher Education.*

Frances has had extensive experience as an early childhood teacher and school administrator, and is currently the president of the National Association of Early Childhood Teacher Educators.

Carol Tureski began her teaching career as a Peace Corps Fellow in the New York City public schools in 1992. She has taught English as a Second Language, humanities, and Spanish in high school classrooms in both Brooklyn and Queens. Her primary interest lies in working with adolescents with low literacy skills. This interest has led to her membership in Brooklyn High School's Project Freire Curriculum Team and participation as a lead teacher in the Freire Saturday School Program.

Carol's strong belief in the need for and power in the collective voice of teachers has led to her involvement in the Teachers Network Policy Institute in which she is a MetLife Fellow. She has found the institute to be a valuable arena for ideas to improve her classroom teaching, schools, and the profession. Ten years into the teaching profession, Carol is continually growing as an educator—either facilitating workshops on young adult literacy or learning a new language.

Adam Urbanski is the president of Rochester (New York) Teachers Association and a vice president of the American Federation of Teachers (AFT). In Rochester, he proposed and designed an internship program for new teachers, a peer review intervention plan, a career ladder, and a homework hotline service for students. Adam is the director of the newly established Teacher Union Reform Network (TURN), aimed at creating a new vision of teachers' unions that supports needed changes in education.

Adam was a trustee of the National Center for Education and the Economy and a senior associate to the National Commission on Teaching and America's Future. He served on AFT's Task Force on the Future of Education and is a recipient of the Phi Delta Kappa Leadership in Education Award (Rochester Chapter, 1983). He also served on the Harvard University, Kennedy School of Government, Executive Session on "Making the System Work for Children in Poverty"; the Federal Department of Education Board of Directors of the Fund for Improvement and Reform of Schools and Teaching; the Advisory Board of Harvard University's National Center for Educational Leadership; the Board of Advisors of "Education for Democracy/International"; the Policy Working Group at the Annenberg Institute for School Reform; the National Board for Professional Teaching Standards; and the National Assessment Governing Board.

Natasha Warikoo After graduating from Brown University with majors in mathematics and the philosophy of science, Natasha taught in New York City's public schools for four years—most recently at Manhattan International High School, a teacher-run high school for recently arrived immigrants and refugees. During her teaching tenure, Natasha participated in school governance as a member of Manhattan International's Coordinating Council and as the school's Student Council Advisor. She spent summers teaching in India and Brazil, and working for the U.S. Department of Education's Office of Bilingual Education and Minority Language Affairs.

Natasha holds a master's degree in education from Harvard's Graduate School of Education, and is currently a doctoral fellow in Harvard's Multidisciplinary Program in Inequality and Social Policy.

Matt Wayne taught for five years in a small middle school in New York City. His primary experience was in English language arts, but he taught history, Spanish, and physical education as well. In addition, Matt has led professional development in New York City and in San Diego. He also has taught undergraduate education classes at Marymount Manhattan College. Matt recently accepted a position as assistant principal at an elementary school in San Francisco's Bay Area.

Matt has been a MetLife Fellow in the Teachers Network Policy Institute for four years. As a MetLife Fellow, he has had the opportunity to work with policymakers on the city, state, and national level. Matt holds a master of arts degree in English education and a master of education degree in public school administration from Teachers College. He enjoys not only teaching language arts in middle school, but also helping his young daughter, Ella, learn how to read.